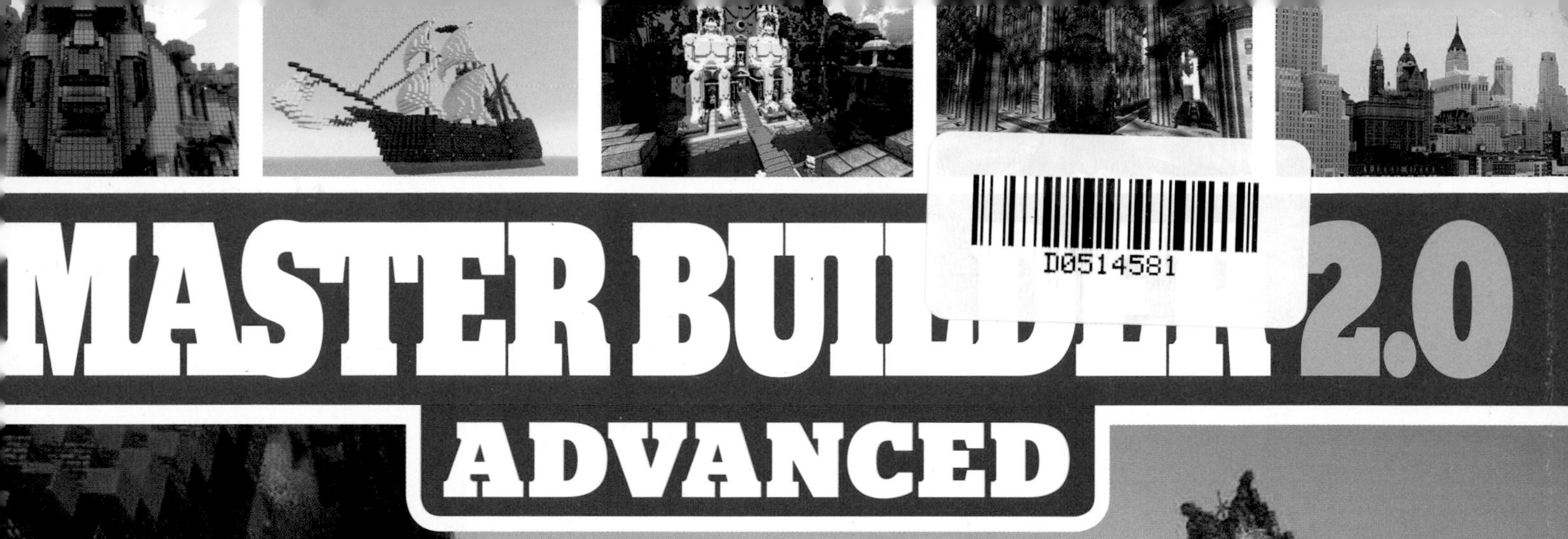

MASTER BUILDER 2.0

ADVANCED

This book is available in quantity at special discounts for your group or organization.
For further information, contact:

Triumph Books LLC
814 North Franklin Street
Chicago, Illinois 60610
Phone: (312) 337-0747
www.triumphbooks.com

Printed in U.S.A.
ISBN: 978-1-62937-265-5

Content packaged by Mojo Media, Inc.
Joe Funk: Editor
Jason Hinman: Creative Director
Trevor Talley and Barry Macdonald: Writers

Contents

Introduction

MINECRAFT! It's everywhere these days, and we here at the Minecrafter absolutely love it. If you hadn't heard of this game before last year, you probably have now, as Minecraft has absolutely exploded onto the public consciousness like few games ever have. Minecraft truly is the king of all indie games, and as one of the most successful and profitable pieces of entertainment ever created, more and more fans are flocking to our favorite blocky builder game all the time. Nowadays it seems just about everyone's getting their mine on!

Because of that overwhelming demand for more!more!more! Minecraft, folks everywhere are looking to learn more about this simple-seeming, but actually extremely complex game. And that, dear Crafters, is where Minecrafter Volume 2 comes in.

Where the first issue of Minecrafter took Crafters from their first steps in the world of the game to basic Redstone and structure building, this jam-packed second issue focuses on more advanced topics and concepts and goes deeper into specific strategies. Want to know how to Kill More Mobs? That's in here. Looking to get a start on a Redstone computer? This guide will put you on the right path. Want to "beat" the game and be the first on your block to read the End Poem without using the Internet? You're about to slay you an Ender Dragon, kiddo!

We've also thrown in more info on the culture of the game outside of actual play in this issue, such as more about Notch and Mojang, Minecon and the various communities that have built up around the game. As Minecraft has grown in popularity, we've started to see some seriously cool stuff go down surrounding the game, and we've collected some excellent data and striking shots to get you up to speed.

Minecrafter Vol. 2 is all about taking you beyond the start of your Minecraft journey and deeper into the game you love (or will soon!). From those who want to build higher, bigger and better, to those who are looking to "beat" this most unconventional of games, to those wanting the newest Redstone tips and tricks, Minecrafter Vol. 2 is your go-to guide for the best strategies, the coolest new structures and every-darn-thing Minecraft there is.

There's a world of infinite imagination and excitement waiting for you just on the other side of this page, so as we say here at the 'Crafter, grab your pickaxe and let's dig in!

State of Minecraft

Before we dive into those tasty, tasty strategies you came to this book for, let's take a moment and look at the state of the Minecraft phenomenon and where it has come in the last year.

{ 12 **million** new copies downloaded in just three years! }

Biggest Year Yet

It's not often that a video game (or anything for that matter) reaches its greatest successes yet nearly five years after originally coming out, but that's exactly what has happened for Minecraft! 2013 was truly Minecraft's year, as not only did the fan-base absolutely explode, but the game itself became much more complex, and there were even two entirely new versions of the game released for the Raspberry Pi and the PlayStation 3!

Speaking of the fans, just take a look at these numbers: It took the PC version of Minecraft from 2009 until January 2011 to be downloaded 1 million times, but as of 2014, the computer version of this much-loved game has now seen an absolutely stunning *13*

million downloads. That's **12 million** new copies downloaded in just three years! The Pocket Edition and Xbox 360 version have equally impressive numbers, with the PE earning 10 million downloads (calculated May 2013) and the Xbox version having been purchased a cool 8 million times (August 2013). Considering that these numbers don't even include the brand-spankin' new PS3 version or the Pi version, not to mention the months since May and August (for the PE and Xbox, respectively), the number of official copies of Minecraft out there is estimated to be over 40 million as of the start of 2014, making it one of the biggest entertainment titles in history.

Two New Platforms to Craft on in 2014

If 2013 was Minecraft's biggest year so far, 2014 looks like it just might rival that title in a big way.

To begin with, Mojang and 4J (the makers of the console ports for the game) have stated that not only will Minecraft continue to be updated for the Xbox and PS3, but that a version will also be released for the new PS4 and Xbox One systems! These versions are said to be compatible with the previous version for each system, meaning players should soon be able to move their Xbox 360 and PS3 worlds onto the newest, most powerful gaming systems on the market.

What to Expect Next

As we've mentioned, this book deals primarily with the two fastest-growing versions of Minecraft (the console and Pocket Editions), and boy-oh-boy is there a lot of new stuff that is set to come out soon for both platforms!

For the PE (Pocket Edition), it's been hinted that an official, working multiplayer version is soon to be released, and we can only hope that such an update will also bring the PE closer to the console, adding more materials, mobs and features.

On the console side, we've already seen one major update since the last Minecrafter, and that added such awesome new features as the Jungle Biome, the fearsome Iron Golem, the adorable Ocelot and new events like Villager breeding and Zombie raids. This may seem like a lot, and it definitely has made the game even more interesting, but it seems that the best is yet to come for the console versions.

Crafter DE4DI3AVES was one of the many to join the game in the last two years

Stained Glass is one thing we expect to see on the console

Among the rumored additions in the upcoming TU14 update for the console are the long-awaited Horses (you can ride 'em!), Withers, Anvils and Hoppers, with some hopeful Minecrafters saying that there's a chance we might see Emerald Ore, Ender Chests, Temples and even trading with Villagers added in. These have all been in the PC version for some time now, and we should see at least a few (if not all of them) on the console in upcoming months.

Speaking of the PC, while this book isn't specifically about that version of the game, we can learn a lot about what's to come for the PE and console versions by looking at what has come out for PC. 2013 saw one of the biggest updates yet to any version of Minecraft with version 1.7.2 for the PC (October). With an absolutely massive amount of new content, including new Mobs, new Biomes and tons of new materials (Stained Glass!), not to mention the

Crafters Sadie and Chloe built this neat blimp in Minecraft PE

awesome new Amplified world type (ravines that go all the way down to the Bedrock!), this update was called The Update that Changed the World, and it shows us that over the next year or so we should continue to get huge amounts of new content added to the other versions of the game.

Where We're At

With all of this (and who knows what else) in store for us from the folks at Mojang, and with Minecraft expanding to just about every major platform out there, this is the most exciting time yet in the world of Minecraft! For you new folks, welcome to one of the most exciting phenomenons and communities in entertainment, while for you veteran Crafters, let's get to work and make even bigger, even better builds. As they say, the sky's the limit in Minecraft.

Cats and Ocelots are some of the most recent additions to the console version of Minecraft

A pair of towers sits atop an Extreme Hills Biome.

What Exactly Do We Mean by "Biome?"

This might seem like an easy question to answer, and in a basic sense, the definition of "Biome" in Minecraft is pretty straightforward: Biomes are the different types of land you can find in Minecraft. However, there are actually two distinct types of Biomes that can be found in the game. For this book, we'll call them "Area Biomes" and "Feature Biomes," respectively, and you'll notice when you play that you'll often find them existing together, with the Feature Biome set within the larger Area Biome.

Area Biomes: We use this term in Minecrafter to refer to the large sections of land that contain certain plants, mobs and aesthetics (for instance, Desert Biomes are mostly yellow and tan with little life, while the Jungle Biome is lush with life and is full of deep greens and browns). When running around the world of Minecraft, Area

Biomes are what you'll most often be in when above ground, and the border between one Area Biome and the next is usually pretty easy to see, as the ground will change color from one Biome to the next. Think of Area Biomes as different types of nature, or environments.

Feature Biomes: Where Area Biomes refer to areas where certain plants and mobs live, Feature Biomes are more recognizable by their shape. Think of them as natural structures, including Beaches, Rivers, Ravines and Hills. Caves aren't technically considered a Biome, but we've included them with Feature Biomes as they have many similarities.

Why You Should Know Your Biomes

Other than the obvious reason that you want to be an ultra-level, super-guru, Minecrafter genius-person, there is an important practical reason that knowing your various Biomes is a great idea: some items, mobs, structures and even Feature Biomes exist mostly or even exclusively in specific Biomes.

For instance, say you're looking for a lot of Wood and you need it really quickly. Well, if you know your Biomes, you know to stay away from the Desert Biome, and hopefully there's a Jungle Biome nearby. Ready to go cave-diving? The Extreme Hills Biome is your best bet, and you're unlikely to find what you're looking for in the Jungle.

The fact that not all Biomes are created equal, and that some contain resources you'll need more often (like Wood) and others don't, also makes it important to know Biomes at the beginning of your game when choosing a spot for a home. There's nothing worse than building a super-sweet house and then realizing that you'll have to hoof it about five minutes to the north to get more Wood because you built your home in a Biome without many trees.

The Biome Breakdown

So now that you know why you'll be an even better Crafter when you get your Biome game on lock-down, let's get into it! While we're not going to get into the crazy math that goes behind each Biome (it's out there online, if you're interested), we are going to give you a basic idea of what each Biome is like, what you can find there, why you might want to visit it and whether or not it's a good spot to build a base. We've simplified the info for the Feature Biomes, as they are more about looks and things don't spawn exclusively in them.

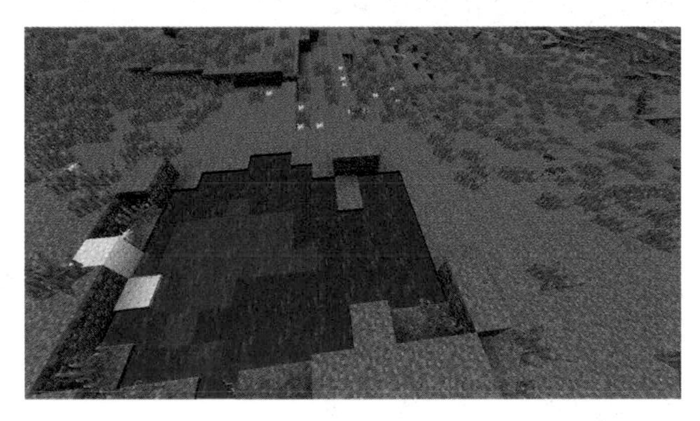

Area Biomes

Plains Biome: What It's Like- One of the more common Biomes, the Plains (or Grasslands) is full of Grass, Flowers and some smaller Trees. It usually features plenty of mobs (both hostile and friendly) roaming about, and you can sometimes find caves, lakes, Villages and Lava pools scattered around it.
Unique Items, Resources and Mobs: None

Reasons to Visit: It's peaceful and has plentiful Grass (for Seeds) and peaceful mobs to hunt. It's also good for later in the game when you have a lot of resources and want a big space to build something in.

Good for a Base? Only on the edges. Building too far into the Plains will lead to lots of time spent running to Forest Biomes and others with more resources, but building on the edges of the Plains can be fun.

Forest Biome

What It's Like: Trees, Trees and more Trees! Another very common Biome, the Forest Biome is one of the most useful early in the game, as they provide large amounts of Wood.

Unique Items, Resources and Mobs:

- Wolves are often found wandering outside of Forest Biomes, but they tend to spawn here.
- Though you can find plenty of Trees elsewhere, the Jungle Biome is the only Biome with a greater concentration of Trees (and those are almost exclusively Jungle Trees).

Reasons to Visit: You need Wood! Also, they are excellent for mob hunting, even in the day, as the shadows created by Trees are ideal for keeping hostile mobs spawned.

Good for a Base? Absolutely! The easy access to wood makes Forests great for your first base, though you might want to find an edge of the Forest so that you don't have to clear out so many leaves.

Desert Biome

What It's Like: Sparse of life and resources, the Desert is pretty cool-looking, but is not a great place to spend large amounts of time unless it is near another, more resource-heavy Biome.

Unique Items, Resources and Mobs:

- Cactus grows in the Desert and can be used for traps and decoration.
- Sand and Sandstone, while not exclusive to the Desert, will be found in the largest amounts here.
- Dry Bushes also grow here and are mostly used for decoration.

Reasons to Visit: The three primary reasons people head to the Desert are Sand, Cactus and Desert Villages. For whatever reason, Villagers love the Desert, and you'll often find a Village or two within. Primarily, however, Deserts are best for grabbing Sand for making Glass and Sandstone.

Good for a Base? Only at the edge of the Desert and another Biome. It's good to have a Desert near your base (as you'll probably want Glass at some point), but its utter lack of trees is a huge drawback for building a base there.

Swamp Biome

What It's Like: Lots of little bits of land surrounded by water. Features short Oak Trees covered in Vines, often has Mushrooms and Lily Pads around.

Unique Items, Resources and Mobs:

- Lily Pads are most commonly found here. These are fun decorations, but you can also build bridges across water with them.

Reasons to Visit: Swamps are okay for Wood, but you're always better off finding a Forest Biome when you need large amounts. Most of the reason players go to Swamps is to find the resources that are common there, such as Lily Pads, Vines and Mushrooms.

Good for a Base? Can be a cool-looking spot for your home, but you'll need to have a Forest nearby in the long-run.

Extreme Hills Biome

What It's Like: You'll know this one when you see it: huge hills with massive cliffs, overhangs and even waterfalls. One of the most interesting-looking Biomes there is, and a fan-favorite.

Unique Items, Resources and Mobs: None as of now (Emerald Ore is exclusive here but not yet included on the console versions of Minecraft).

Reasons to Visit: When looking for caves and resources, this is by far your best bet. Extreme Hills Biomes are absolutely riddled with cave openings, and because there's so much exposed rock, you'll often be able to simply look around outside for Coal and Iron Ore.

Good for a Base? Again, yes, but only if there's a Forest nearby. One trick is to start at a Forest, collecting a lot of Wood and Saplings, and then move to a nearby Extreme Hills Biome to build your home. As they're great for caves, it helps you later in the game, and you can always plant your Saplings on the Extreme Hills (which looks awesome too).

Mushroom Island Biome

What It's Like: Maybe the most unique Biome, this features purple-ish Mycelium as its primary building block and has Huge Mushrooms that look like trees. Always found out in the Ocean Biome.

Unique Items, Resources and Mobs:

- Mycelium, a unique Dirt-like building block that is purple/grey and which Mushrooms like to grow on.
- Mooshrooms hang out on the Mushroom Island. These are Cows that have Mushrooms growing on them. These are great food sources, as you can get Milk, Beef, Mushrooms and Mushroom Stew from them, as well as Leather.
- Giant Mushrooms are another great food source, as chopping them down gives you large amounts of Mushrooms.

Reasons to Visit: For one, there are no hostile mobs on these islands, so they're nice as sanctuaries. They're also very good for food, and if you can manage to get a Mooshroom back to your base, you'll have a constant plentiful food source.

Good for a Base? Nope. You could always build a secondary base on one, or a bridge or tunnel connecting your base to one, but because they are so isolated out in the water, you're going to constantly have to go back to the main landmass to get other resources.

Taiga Biome

What It's Like: Can often be snowy and is a sort-of "Russian"-style forest with Spruce Trees and Wolves.

Unique Items, Resources and Mobs:

- Another great place to find Wolves (though again, they aren't unique to here).
- The best bet for Spruce Trees

Reasons to Visit: Mostly just to chop down Spruce Trees or find Wolves to tame.

Good for a Base? Can be, though you'll be stuck with just one Wood type for the most part. Mostly good for raiding for Spruce Wood.

Jungle Biome

What It's Like: BIIIIG Trees. Like, really, really big Trees. And lots of them. Tons of foliage in general, and usually some hilly areas and lakes.

Unique Items, Resources and Mobs:

- Jungle Trees. These are absolutely the best Wood resource out there, and you'll love finding a Jungle just to get at these giant Trees. They can be as big as four times wider than a normal Tree and many, many times taller. You'll often find them covered in Vines as well.
- Cocoa Pods are sometimes found on Jungle Trees and are used in food crafting.
- Ocelots! One of the cutest and most useful mobs, the Ocelot is very hard to catch but when tamed they can be used as pets or as guards against Creepers (that's right, Creepers hate Cats and won't go near 'em!)

Reasons to Visit: Get on top of Jungle Tree and chop down all the Wood you'll ever need (well, for about a project or so at least). You'll also want Cats at some point to protect your stuff, so Ocelot taming is a good reason as well.

Good for a Base? Sure! With all that Wood around, why not try a tree-house? You'll probably need to visit others for certain resources, but the Jungle is a great Biome for building, if you can clear out a spot.

Ocean Biome

What It's Like: Lots and lots of water, going off into the distance. There are also underwater caves and Squids!

Unique Items, Resources and Mobs:

- Squids can sometimes find their ways into Rivers, but you're mostly gonna find these neat little guys (that drop Ink Sacs) in the Ocean.

Reasons to Visit: If you're feeling adventurous and want to try an underwater cave, or if you need a Squid. They can also be pretty good for taking a Boat around, as you can explore the coast.

Good for a Base? Not at all. The Ocean has zero Wood and is hard to build in, not to mention breathe. Of course, everyone wants to have an underwater base at some point, so if you've got the resources, it's a fun place for a secondary home later in the game.

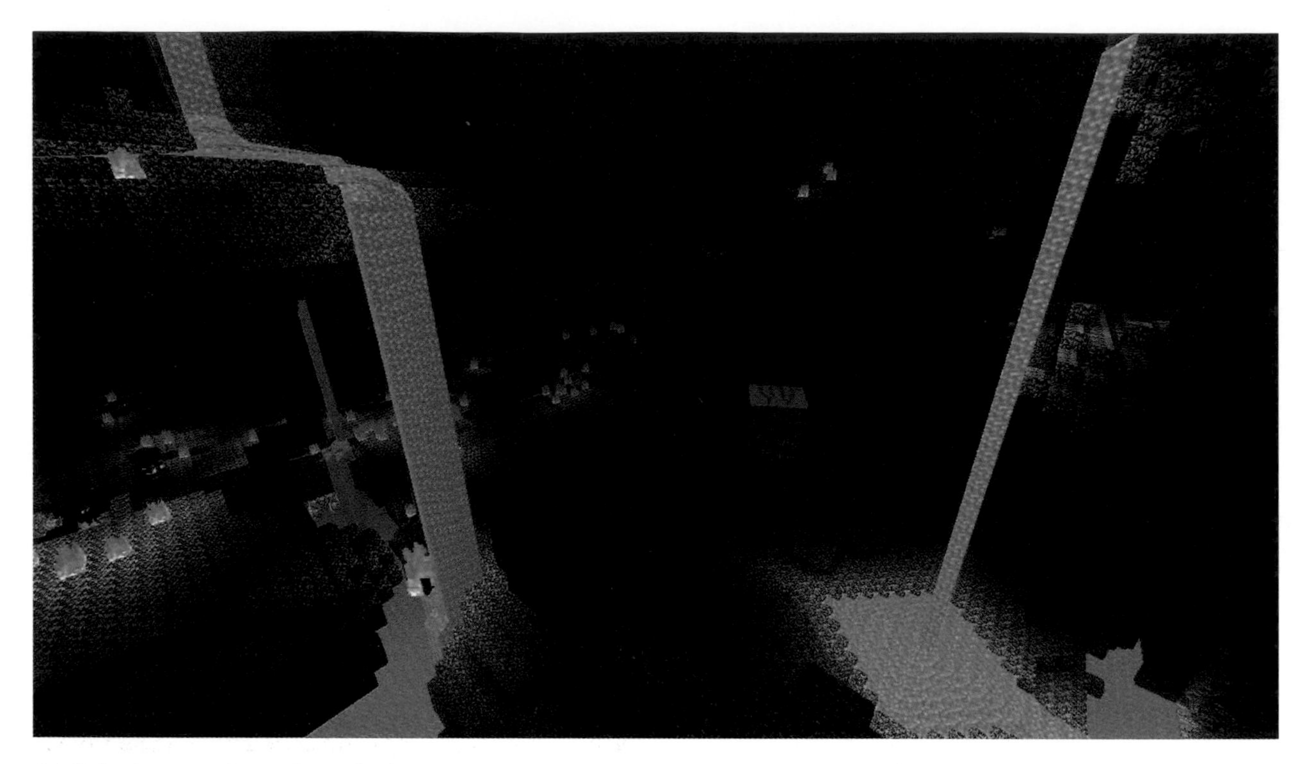

Of all the Biomes, the Nether is by far the most dangerous. That also makes it one of the most fun, however!

Nether Biome

What It's Like: Fire, Lava, things trying to kill you constantly, little in the way of food. Basically super, super hostile.

Unique Items, Resources and Mobs: TONS. The Nether is like a whole new world, and most of what you'll find there is exclusive.

- Nether Rack is a red building block that when set on fire stays on fire.
- Nether Brick is made from Nether Rack and has a similar relationship to Stone's relationship to Cobblestone.
- Soul Sand is a building block that makes things move slow, great for docks for your Boat.
- Glowstone is a building block that produces light.
- Nether Wart is a plant resource that is used in recipes and only found in the Nether
- Magma Cubes are like Slimes, but made of fire and Lava and are pretty darn dangerous.
- Ghasts are huge, flying creatures that shoot fireballs and will seriously mess you up.
- Zombie Pigmen are passive, unless you attack them, and they wield weapons.
- Blazes are some of the more dangerous mobs, floating around and shooting Fire Charges at you. You'll need to kill some at some point if you want to make it to The End.

Reasons to Visit: Besides all of the unique resources, the mobs and the unique things they drop, you'll need to get to the Nether to get items you need to get to The End.

Good for a Base? You can try, but Beds explode on placement in the Nether, so don't expect to get too comfy. Take Stone and Cobblestone with you, as you're going to need something to protect you from Ghast blasts.

Feature Biomes

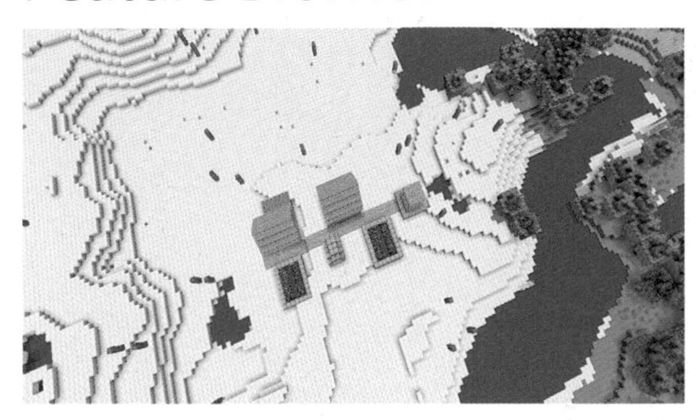

River Biome

What It's Like: Neat little rivers, cutting through the land and giving it definition.

Reasons to Visit: They look very cool, and it's always fun to build near one.

Hills Biome

What It's Like: Just plain ole hills, these can occur on many Biomes including Desert, Plains and Forests.

Reasons to Visit: Good for building on top of, as they offer a view of the surrounding mobs at night.

Ravine Biome

What It's Like: Giant gashes cut into the land that go down very, very far. These can be on the surface or underground, and can often contain waterfalls and Lava falls.

Reasons to Visit: They can be neat to build across or on either side of, but mostly they are just spectacular for getting ore and finding caves, as you can just look at the wall and see where the deposits are.

Beach Biome

What It's Like: Little bits of Sand on the edge of water.

Reasons to Visit: Mostly just for Sand, and sometimes they have Clay as well!

Feature Biomes

Cave Biome

What It's Like: Winding, often-complex tunnels through the ground, full of hostile mobs.

Reasons to Visit: These are your best-bet for running into the best resources and structures in the game (like Diamond, Redstone, Fortresses and Abandoned Mineshafts). You'll be spending a lot of time in caves, and it's a good idea to find one very big one and build a little base in it to explore from.

Deep Ocean Biome

What It's Like: The Ocean Biome, except with massive underwater mountains and Ravines.

Reasons to Visit: Same as the Ocean Biome, but good for giant underwater structures.

"Snowy" Biomes

What It's Like: Many Biomes have "cold" or "Snowy" versions where you can find Ice and Snow, as well as get actual snow-falling animations. Plains, Taiga, Rivers and Beaches can all have "Snowy" versions.

Reasons to Visit: You can get Snowballs here, which can be turned into Snow Blocks. Ice is also fun to use, as you slip across it, and the "Snowy" Biomes just look plain awesome.

{ "Infinite power just isn't very interesting, no matter what game you're playing. It's much more fun when you have a limited tool set to use against the odds. Usually, a new player to Minecraft doesn't make it through the first night. They're just not prepared for the danger. It's a harsh lesson but it establishes the rules."

— Notch on why Minecraft is the way it is }

A Jungle Biome sits just above a Cave Biome, giving this area a quite cool look.

Kill More Mobs

Thing is, when you play Minecraft in Survival mode, some creature at some point in the game will attempt to kill you, and it will succeed. We all know this when we start a world (which typically involves dying once or five times), but after a while you get comfy in your safe house and well-lit mine, and you forget that outside your cozy walls lies death. And then it comes for you, in the form of a sizzling Creeper you didn't see until it was too late, or a nest of Cave Spiders that you suddenly crack into, and you're dead. All your gear is probably lost, you're far from where you were, and then you remember: combat happens in Minecraft. **Let's get you ready to fight.**

1. Prepare for Battle, Young Miner

Nothing you do in Minecraft is more important to your success in combat than preparation. Every good strategy involves at least some of it, and it is the core of almost all successful offense and defense. Fail to prepare, or at least think ahead a bit, and you're gonna die. Do even the smallest bit of prep work, and you're gonna kill some mobs, kiddo.

So let's get you prepared. These are far from the only ways to prepare in this game, but they'll at least get you set on the path to tasty triumph over the dark forces that wait outside the walls of your home.

Crafter Robot Noise is decked out in enchanted armor and a Diamond Sword, ready for battle.

You'll notice the difference that Diamond gear makes right away. There really is no substitute.

Eat This, Not That

Best before battle:

- Golden Apple
- Cooked Porkchop
- Steak

Good before battle:

- Cooked Chicken
- Mushroom Stew
- Bread
- Cooked Fish

Bad before battle:

- Apple
- Melon
- Uncooked meat
- Cookie

Light up the area around your base. Hostile mobs only spawn where the light level is low. When you leave your base unlit, you're letting the mobs choose when to fight you. Turn the tables by lighting the area around your base, that way you only fight on your terms.

It's okay to spend on gear. We know, we know— you want to save that Diamond for <insert difficult to acquire item here>. Well, we get that, but trust us on this one. The amount of lesser materials you will save by spending that Iron or Diamond on good Armor and weapons is going to make that enchanted Diamond Sword pay for itself. You won't just die less, you'll die a lot less, and your ability to kill mobs quickly will result in experience and drops galore.

A miner's gotta eat. Food is the most often forgotten and perhaps most important part of combat. Health regeneration and the ability to sprint (and thus knock the mob back, aka "knockback") depend on your continuing to have a full food bar (the bar with the meat-on-bones). Eat foods that have good hunger-to-saturation restoration levels before battle for best effects, and avoid those with low hunger-to-sat. You should also bring such foods with you when going out hunting and eat them whenever hungry. Keeping yourself well-fed with the right foods all throughout your combat period is essential.

This pit and staircase combo is an excellent build for mob hunting, as it allows you to shoot from on top of it, drawing mobs toward you and hopefully into the pit. Make it even better by building a fence and a gate at the back.

Prepare the land. Make the battlefield your own, not just with lights, but with traps, murder holes and more. The thrill of attacking blind is great at times, but if you're looking to become a true hunter, take the daylight hours to prepare your hunting grounds for maximum success. Create pits, holes and cliffs to lead or knock mobs into and know where they are. Build tunnels and places to attack from above (little towers and forts) that you can access but keep you safe from mobs. This is where you can start to have the most fun with hunting (and essentially farming) mobs, and where you can get the most creative. Turn the area around your base into a place that invites mobs in, murders them brutally and leaves the spoils for you to collect.

2. Offense Is the Best Offense

When combat comes, and it will, don't go swinging blindly. And in fact, don't just swing. The Minecraft community has come up with a few tried and true methods that will amplify your ability to come out of a mob encounter on the life-having end by enormous amounts, and you'll find they'll lead to a lot fewer frantic trips back to your dropped pile of loot.

Sprint and hit to get a knockback. Attacking a mob at sprint causes you to knock it back. This is good for two reasons: It puts distance between you and the mob, and it gives you the opportunity to knock them off of something and damage them. This is especially useful when you know or have prepared the battleground.

Circle around while attacking: the circle strafe. One of Minecraft's two most trusted attack styles, circle strafing involves putting an enemy in the center of your vision while you walk around them in a circle, attacking the whole time. Called the circle strafe, this method makes it hard for most enemies to attack while giving you the opportunity to do damage. NOTE: does not work on Creepers unless you're just crazy good at it.

Flint & Steel

Is, in fact, so useful in combat that it should be considered second most essential to a Sword.

Attack, pull back and draw them in, attack again: kiting. Kiting is the second of the two sacred Minecraft combat strategies. "Kiting a mob" is when you hit a mob and then back away while keeping your vision focused on the mob. Mobs immediately attack after you hit them, so by pulling away, you can direct them toward you (as if you were pulling them on a kite string). As your target comes to attack, time a second attack perfectly so that they are hit and knocked back a bit, giving you the chance to back away again and repeat the process. Kiting is one of the safer and most effective strategies in Minecraft combat, and it can be used in combination with archery as well as with traps for seriously damaging attacks.

- Swords aren't your only weapons. The best hunters use all of their tools. Swords are the primary weapon, but you can also light blocks on fire with Flint and Steel, drop Lava, suffocate with Gravel or Sand (you have to time those just right), drown with Water and even slow mobs down with Cobwebs or Soulsand. Try all of these in combat at least once and arm yourself with the weapons you are best at using.

3. Keeping Alive: Defense in Minecraft

While prepping and attacking correctly are great, sometimes you just need to stay alive to win the fight. And, let's be honest, sometimes you just need to stay alive period. Don't let your first thirty deaths get ya down, Crafters: staying alive can be done, and done well.

Putting a wall between the Crafter and the Creeper will save you over and over.

Putting Torches down while attacking ensures that mobs won't spawn in this exact area again (though they might be able to travel there).

This angry Spider can't get to his attacker when he's underwater!

Use the zigzag method. Most mobs do not do well with direction change when it comes to attacking (the Silverfish being a definite exception). Skeletons in particular just can't handle it, so whether you're attacking or running away, strafing from side to side will boost your chances of success.

Put blocks between you and them. Mobs will chase you, but if you make a move when they can't see you, they won't know you did it. This means that getting behind something and then changing direction or tactics can save your butt more often than not. This is great for attacking, but even better when you need to get yourself out of combat quickly.

Go underwater. No mob can swim to try and kill you underwater, so if you need to get away, dive down, kid.

Spam those torches. Remember, mobs will keep spawning anywhere there is darkness, and if mobs have put you in a bad situation in one spot on the map once, they probably will do so again unless you do something. Spamming torches on the environment when running is a great preventative measure for now and the future.

Any good general will tell you: always take the higher ground when possible.

4. Generally Good Ideas

Just plain smart things to think about when it comes to Minecraft huntin'.

Creepers start their countdown when you are within three blocks and end it when you leave the three block range. That might sound like pretty specific advice, but anyone who's played the game much at all knows that no other mob really compares to the Creeper when it comes to doin' damage. Know this fact and use it to your advantage.

With full health, this Zombie should be no problem. If this Miner was hurtin', however, it would be best to avoid combat in this dark tunnel.

Don't Fight Unless You Can and Want to. You don't have to prove your bravery in Minecraft. Fighting when you are close to death, don't have good gear, are far from home or are otherwise unprepared leads to death, which leads to losing precious items and time. Run away first, fight when the odds are in your favor, and your game will progress a whole lot faster than that of your "brave" friends.

5. Colonel Creeperkiller's Strategy Corner

Okay we made that name up, but this neat little strategy section needed a flashy title. Pulled from the deep depths of the Crafter community, these specific strategies should be learned and used when you find yourself in a tough spot. When you get good at them all and combine them with the above tips, you'll find yourself wrecking your way through wave after endless wave of mobs, reaping their delicious experience orbs and laughing as you stand tall as the apex predator of the Minecraft world. Or something like that. NOTE: These tricks can be used on mobs or, if you're feeling rascally, on other players.

By digging above this Zombie, he has no idea he's about to die.

Getting past mobs in tunnels is a great use of the Ender Pearl (if you can afford to use one).

When a Creeper's coming head-on like this, the best option is to get around him and hit from behind.

The Duck and Swing. Best on mobs, make the mob lose sight of you, then move to attack mode. Basically, move to a place where the mob can't see you. They will continue to come at the last place they saw you, so you can move yourself to a place where you can attack them. Swing around behind or above, and you'll have the advantage on the unsuspecting mob. This strategy is super tricky in PVP, but it feels pretty great when you pull it off.

The Reverse Sapper. Tunnel above enemies or mobs and unleash your fury. Don't feel confined to the way the environment is set up. If you know where they'll be, dig so that you pop up just above them and rock them with attacks. One of the most effective strategies there is.

Ender Bouncing. Pretty straightforward, but expensive: throw Enderpearls to teleport around the battlefield. Especially effective when you throw them through throw walls of fire or where enemies can't see/reach, gaining you a tactical advantage.

A Creeper's about to learn what the Pit Knock is.

The Mini Murder Fort from a distance.

Stack your Mini Murder Fort with some useful items.

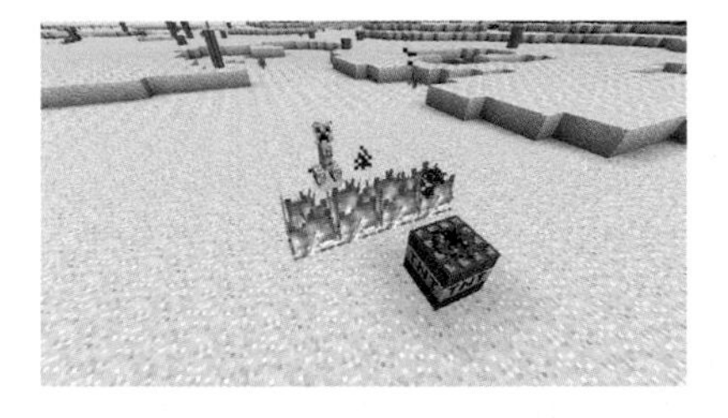

Finn Fu done correctly is devastating.

The hilarious Sato Technique about to make a Creeper pay.

The Pit Knock. Set up a pit that's either deep enough to damage anything that falls in it or that has something damaging in it like Cactus or fire. Lure enemies near it and knock 'em in with a sprint attack or a weapon with the Knockback enchantment. Mob falls in, collect loot at the bottom, profit. Can also be made more complicated by creating a drowning or suffocating trap (see the Inventions section).

The Murder Hole. Create a border around a part of your base where you leave one block open just above where the ground level is on the outside of the base. On the inside of the base, make this spot accessible so that it is at your head-height. This will make it so you can attack the feet of mobs, while most can't get to you. Spiders, however, still sometimes can. Stinkin' Spiders.

The Mini Murder Fort. Get yourself all geared up and find a good spot out in the wild during the day where mobs are likely to spawn at night. Build yourself a little spot where you can reach mobs on all sides but they have a hard time getting to you. This can either be slightly up in the air or slightly underground (or both, for The Ultra Mini Murder Fort), putting you just out of reach of most mobs. Wait til dark, and then wreck all that dare come near. Even Spiders will usually just jump on top, and if you have a one-block hole punched in the ceiling, you'll have a fine window to kill them through.

Finn Fu. Start a ranged attack on an enemy with a Bow, then create a large firewall on a line of blocks in front of you using Flint and Steel. The enemy can't see through the fire, so drop TNT blocks behind it. Pull away from the firewall, shooting through it at the enemy. If hit, the enemy will usually kite, following you through the firewall. This will light them on fire, running them into the TNT and blowing them up. Works even better if you can put it in a pit and then escape out of the top of it. NOTE: Most items and blocks are destroyed by TNT. You will probably still find some resources that were hit with the shock-wave, however.

The Sato Technique. Set a TNT trap by digging down two blocks and placing one TNT block at the bottom of the pit. Put a block that can take a Pressure Plate above the TNT and put a Pressure Plate on it. Now kite a mob or enemy over the plate, and if you can keep them in the general vicinity, they'll go sky-high when the TNT detonates. Also works best in a pit. NOTE: Also destroys most items. But is really, really funny. Can also be used as a trap around your base, but not too close of course (unless you've got an Obsidian blast wall).

Advanced Redstone & Inventions

If getting to 'The End' is the culmination of the adventure part of Minecraft, being able to incorporate Redstone into your builds is the pinnacle of construction. This is easier said than done, as Redstone and its mechanisms are basically a fully functioning system of electric power and circuitry, and a truly complete knowledge of the feature is almost impossible (even the guys who build computers out of it always have something else to learn).

Despite that, graduating from basic Lever-and-Door setups isn't all that hard, and learning the basic building blocks of various systems that can be combined into more complex builds shouldn't be hard for most player who give it a go.

In order to get your wheels turning and start the path to your Redstone mastery, here are some projects to try out in your worlds. We'll start with the simple fun of a few traps before we move on to some of the basic circuit types.

Traps

A good trap setup correctly and activated at the right time is one of the best things in Minecraft. Seeing a Creeper unsuspectingly step on a rigged plate before exploding, or tricking another player into falling to their doom is thoroughly rewarding, and they're experiences you're likely to have when you build one of these bad boys.

Death Wall

You don't have to leave your house to murder mobs. The Death Wall turns your house into a death-dispensing fortress controlled by just a Lever and a little Redstone, and it's not too hard to set up.

This trap takes advantage of the fact that a Dispenser filled with an Arrow stack will fire its Arrows when powered. While you can always just leave some full Dispensers lying about your map with a Pressure Plate in front of them (so they attack the mob that steps on them), you're unlikely to do a whole lot of damage this way. Instead, incorporate the concept into your home by placing Dispensers in your walls facing outward. Put a stack or two of Arrows in these and connect all Dispensers to one Lever in your house with Redstone.

If you get it wired up right, the Dispensers will fire a volley of Arrows at whatever is in front of them when you flip the Lever. Flip it off and then on again, and they'll fire again, and you can repeat the action until the Arrows run out. This is actually faster than Buttons, and is quite devastating.

This is easiest when the back of the Dispensers are exposed on the inside wall of your house, but if you play around with burying your Redstone lines, you can create some highly destructive firing patterns with Dispensers shooting across the land outside your base from various angles. This method is also one of the better PVP defense mechanisms, though players can always steal arrows from your Dispensers.

Simple TNT traps are fun and also quite funny, though only beginner players will be fooled by them.

Miner's First TNT Trap

TNT traps are without question the most popular way for miners to get a trick kill on other miners, and though they're not great when it comes to keeping dropped loot intact, they are some of the most entertaining things to build in the game. On top of, and perhaps because of that, players have gotten ridiculously creative over the years with various styles of TNT traps, but almost everybody starts with one basic trap.

That is the Pressure Plate TNT trap, the most basic explosive trap in the game. All it takes is digging a hole two blocks deep, then putting a TNT block at the bottom. Put a block of another material on top of the TNT block, and then put a Pressure Plate on that. When players run over, a few seconds later the area will blow up.

Now, you'll probably catch a few players here and there with this simple version of the trap, but because it takes a few seconds and players usually run away, not to mention that it's pretty easy to see the Pressure Plate, this trap is too basic to kill most players or mobs. Luckily, it's one of the easiest to tweak with more TNT, more Redstone, or disguises for the trap, so just play around with it!

Note how the Torches keep the Sand from falling. Using this method, you can create a Sand floor of any shape that can be taken out by just one piston.

Fake Floor of Hilarity

If you place a Torch on a block, you can then place another block on the space above the first block, and then place a block of Sand or Gravel on the space above the Torch. Since this block of Sand or Gravel doesn't have an actual block below it (just a Torch), it would usually fall, but the Torch keeps it up. By combining this feature with the fact that a layer of Sand will fall if the layer supporting it falls, we can create one of the most dramatic and funny traps in the game, the Fake Floor of Hilarity.

You'll want to check out the photos for this one, because it's a little different than the kinds of builds many players are used to. Essentially what happens is that a player walks over a Pressure Plate to open an Iron Door to a room (a Chest on the far wall can help to entice players). As they walk into the room, the Iron Door slams shut behind them, and they get stuck as there is no way to open the Door from the inside. Before they can decide to break out, the Sand floor beneath their feet suddenly starts collapsing until the entire floor has fallen out of the room and down a huge pit, taking the player with them.

Here's a basic breakdown of what you need to do to create this tricky fake room: first dig a big pit that's either far enough down to kill or do big damage to the tricked player (or that has something damaging at the bottom like Cactus, fire etc.). In the middle of the pit, build a one-block tower of Sand up out of the pit to at least 6 blocks below ground level. Now put Torches on each side of the top block on the tower. Make the tower one block of Sand taller, and then put blocks of Sand on all sides of that block. Because the Torches are below, they will stay in place despite having no block beneath them. You can then put Torches on the sides of the new layer of Sand blocks and repeat with a third layer.

You'll have to bury the Redstone, of course, but this exposed view shows how the Pressure Plate is wired to both the Iron Door and the Redstone below, which leads to the Piston.

By repeating this process and placing Torches and blocks in the right place, you can eventually create a flat rectangle of Sand that can be used as a floor (or another shape, if you want). Then, build a room of some sturdy, regular building material around the Sand floor, adding an Iron Door as the only entrance.

If you calculate this right so that the floor of Sand is about level with the ground outside, and if you put it in an area where a Sand floor doesn't seem weird, you're very likely to trick other players into thinking that they've come across a normal room. Adding items like a Chest across from the Door in a little alcove in the wall, or maybe some items set on the Sand or walls, will also help draw in the unsuspecting.

But before you can trap your friends with your sweet, sweet fake house, you need to wire it up with Redstone. This is pretty simple: start with a Pressure Plate in front of the Iron Door and then put a Piston up against one of the blocks on the one block tower that holds up your fake floor. Wire the Piston to the Pressure Plate (make sure this is hidden) so that stepping on the Plate opens the Door and also makes the Piston shove one of the blocks out of the supporting one-block-wide tower.

Because of the way Sand (and Gravel) acts, the first block falling out of the supporting tower causes the block of Sand above it to fall as well, which causes anything supported by it to fall as well. The resulting chain reaction means each level above the block that the Piston shoved will fall one by one, eventually causing the entire floor to collapse into the pit below it. At this point anyone who has entered your house is either dead, or at the least very hurt and stuck in a pit with nothing to show for it.

The House Cleaner in cut-away. See how it starts with a small amount of Water that is spread by the Stone below.

This is the kind of pattern that you should use to spread the stream of Water.

The House Cleaner

One of the neater projects we've ever seen in person was a system that used Water and Redstone to clean out an entire house whenever a Lever was pulled, and this really isn't too hard to set up in smaller homes or those that plan it out from the get-go. When it comes to counteracting home invasions, whether of the mob or other player sort, The House Cleaner is among the best, as it's quick, doesn't mess up most of your stuff and can be turned off easily.

To build, start pretty high above the rooms you want your system to flood. Build a trench three blocks long and two blocks deep, then remove one of the blocks at the bottom of one end of the trench. Two blocks away from this, place a Sticky Piston so that it's facing where the block was, and then attach a block to it. Wire this Piston up with Redstone to a Lever in a spot in your house that will be safe from the Water, so that when you flip the Lever the Piston pushes the block it is attached to back into the bottom of the trench, closing the hole.

At the top of the other end of the Trench, drop a Water Bucket so that the Water flows through the trench and down out the hole when the Piston is pulled back. When you flip the Lever so the Piston moves forward again, it should then close the hole in the trench, blocking the flow of Water.

Under the hole in the trench, leave a few blocks, and then place five blocks in the shape of a cross (one in the center with a block on all sides). Four or five blocks below this, build a rectangular structure of blocks with holes in it every other block (a kind of honeycomb shape, see picture). When you pull the Lever and the hole opens in the trench, the Water will flow out of the hole and hit the blocks built below it, splitting the flow into multiple flows and widening it so that it can clean out entire rooms.

Building this for one room is easy (just make the flow as wide as the room), allowing you to turn the switch on and off so that the Water flows through and then drains out very quickly. Building it for a complex structure or your whole base will take a lot more work and will involve a great deal of planning, but it can be done, and it ends up being a very useful and fun addition to your build.

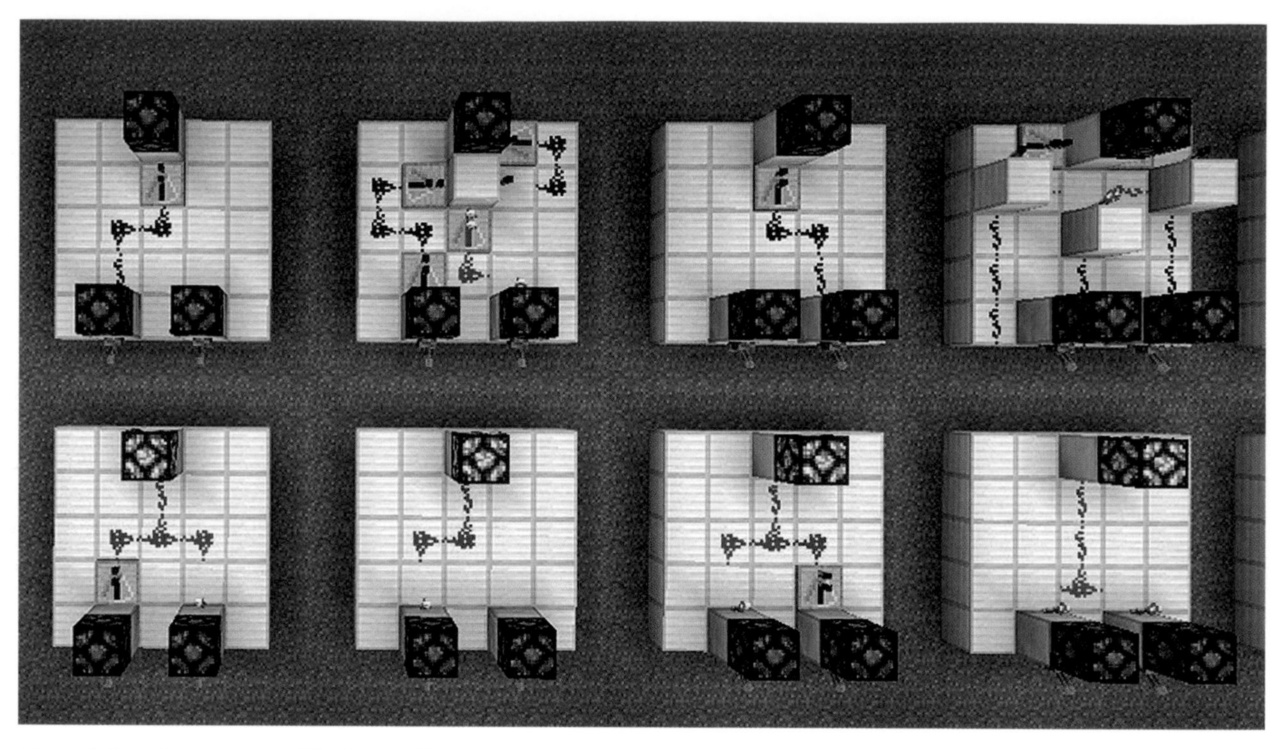

Most of the primary types of Redstone Gates.

Useful Redstone Circuitry

The preceding builds are all a lot of fun and take a bit of Redstone know-how, but neither the builds in this version of Minecrafter nor those in the last even come close to encompassing all that can be done with this powerful game feature. Learning all of the things Redstone can do is really not that different at all from learning how real electronic currents, wiring and even programming work, and some Redstone builds are so complex that you literally need a degree to understand what's going on.

That being said, there are some fairly simple Redstone structures (called "circuits") that are essentially the building blocks for more complex Redstone builds, and by learning them and using them together, you'll be be able to amplify the quality and scope of your Redstone achievements many times over.

NOTE: Interestingly, these "circuits" work almost exactly the same in real life wiring and computing as they do with Redstone, and they've all been around for a very long time.

NOT Gate

The NOT Gate is the simplest advanced Redstone circuit, and it has a very useful function: it reverses the effect of a powered line. So say you have a Piston attached to a Lever: add a NOT Gate between the Piston and the Lever, and instead of making the Piston extend when the Lever is flipped and the Redstone line is powered, it makes the Piston pull back. This is incredibly useful when used on Redstone wires that branch, as you can make one Lever, Button or other such feature do different things to different mechanisms (like make one door open and another close).

To build the NOT Gate, put a Lever down and then a Redstone wire going out from it one block. After the wire, place a block down on the same line as the Lever and the wire are on. On the opposite side of the block to the Lever, place a Redstone Torch. On the block past the Torch (still on line with the Lever for this first one, though you can change it in later builds when you've got the hang of it), place another Redstone wire and then connect this to whatever mechanism you want. When you flip the lever, it will power the wire, which will turn off the Redstone Torch, leaving the mechanism without power. Flip it again, Torch comes back on, mechanism functions.

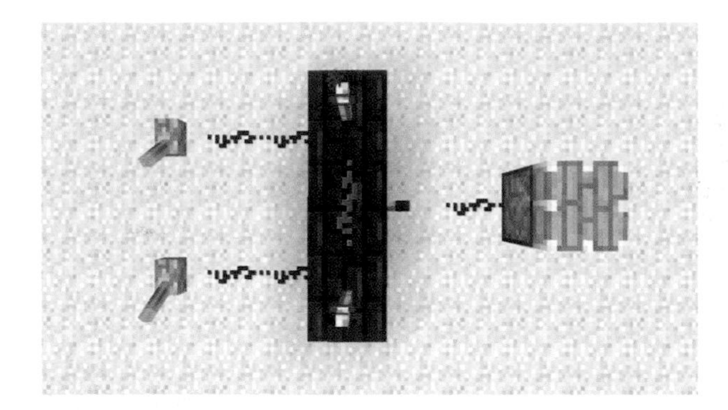

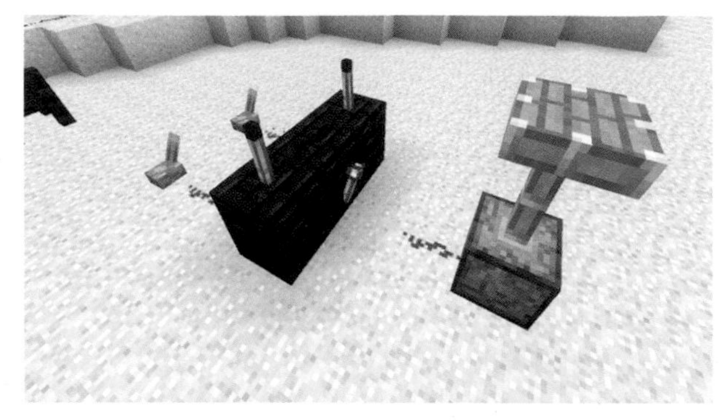

AND Gate

The second type of gate, and perhaps the one you'll hear about most often when players are talking about complex builds, is the AND Gate. Where the NOT gate reverses the power of a Redstone wire, the AND Gate is used to tell a mechanism that it can't function unless two power sources are functioning on it. This means if the AND Gate is attached to two Levers, both must be turned on for the signal to send to the mechanism beyond.

To build, start with two Levers set down going the same direction with Redstone wires coming off of each, also going the same direction (so there should be one block of space between the wires. At the end of each wire, place a block and then place a block between those two. There should now be a line of three blocks , two Redstone wires coming out of the two end blocks, and two Levers on the other side of the wires. On top of the blocks you just placed, put a Redstone Torch at either and and then a Redstone wire between the Torches. On the other side of the blocks from the Levers, pace a Redstone Torch on the side of the middle block. On the block on the ground in front of that third Redstone Torch, place another wire down, and then a mechanism after that.

When a switch is thrown, it sends a current through the wire in front of it to one of the Redstone Torches on top of the blocks and turns it off. If both of these are turned off, the Redstone wire between the two Redstone Torches on top of the block goes underpowered, which turns on the Redstone Torch on the side of the blocks. This then powers the line on the other side of the blocks from the Levers. Turn either Lever off, and the signal does not get through.

Other Gates

There are many types of Redstone circuits and gates out there, with some of the most prominent being the NAND (NOT Gate + AND Gate), the OR Gate (functions if either power source is on, but not if both are), the NOR Gate, the XOR Gate and the NXOR, and all of them are incredibly useful for advance builds. In fact, knowing when and how to use these gates is what really sets the master players apart, and they fittingly can take a very long time to become good at.

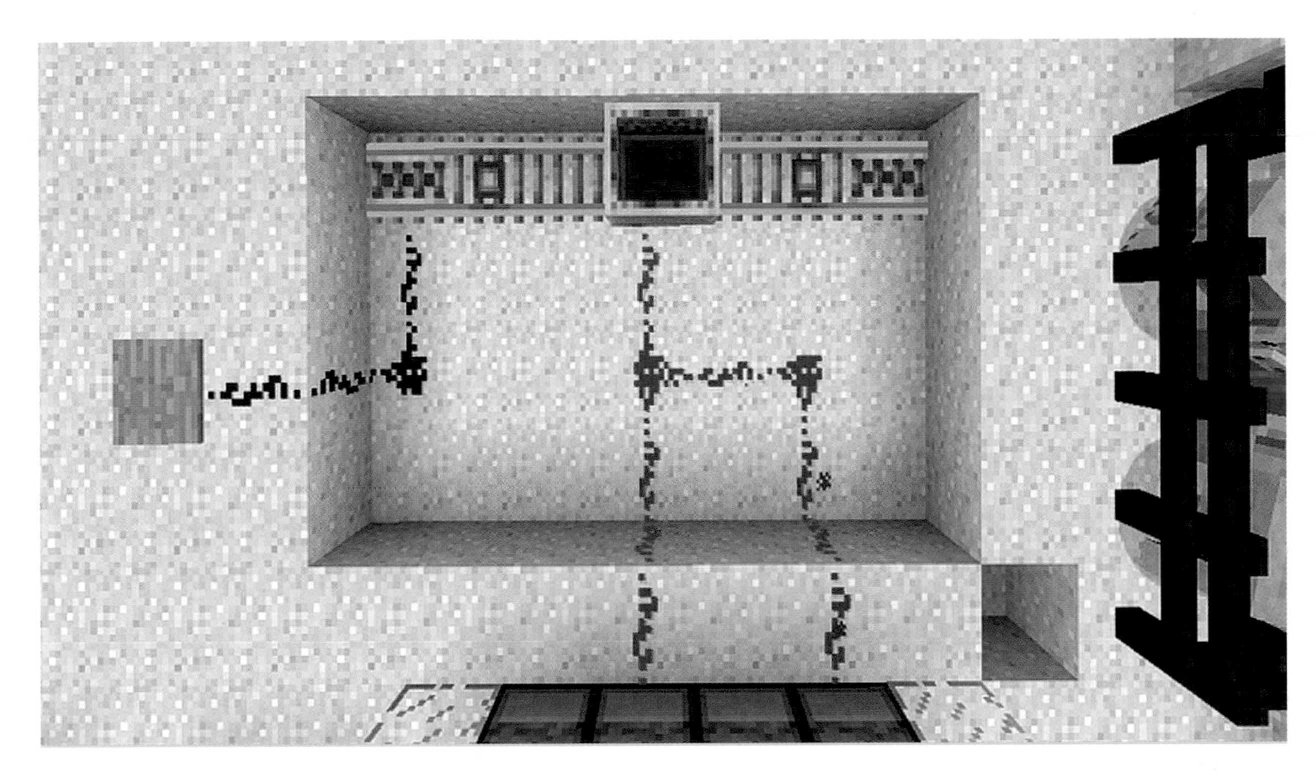

Repeating Signal

Rails, especially Powered Rails and Detector Rails, are also very important when it comes to building advanced Redstone circuits. This is because of the fact that Minecarts take time to travel over Rails, but they can also run over Detector Rails and thus send a signal, so you can use Rails and Minecarts to cause signals to happen at certain times.

There are many, many Rail and Minecart circuits out there, some of which get seriously complex, but here's a fun and easy one to get you started. It's a very quick system that, when built and started up, sends a steady pulsing signal through a Redstone circuit forever until part of the system is destroyed.

Setup requires that you dig an area down that is seven blocks long, one block deep and at least two blocks wide. Lay down a straight line of Rail in this pattern: Powered Rail-Detector Rail-Regular Rail-Detector Rail-Regular Rail-Detector Rail-Power Rail. Lead a Redstone wire from the Detector Rail in the center of the track to whatever mechanism you want to power, as this is where the signal will come from. Attach a second Redstone wire to one of the Powered Rails, and attach that to a Lever or Button. Place a Minecart on that end of the track, and when you flip the Lever, it will send the Minecart going along the track, hitting the Detector Rails in the process.

Because there is a Detector and Power Rail at each end of the track, the Minecart will keep bouncing from one end of the track to the other forever, hitting the Detector in the middle every time and sending a signal from it in a pulsing pattern.

This is very, very useful for automated processes and for complex Redstone circuits in advanced builds, and if you start messing with Redstone quite a bit, it's likely you'll find a use for it in no time flat.

Mine Better

When it's time to slam a Pickaxe into some Stone, you need to be ready to go. There's gonna be a lot going on out there in your mine, from caves to explore, to mobs that'll attack you, to ore to snag and more, and it's easy to get distracted (and killed). Remember miner: when you put Pickaxe into hand and you set out for ore, you've got one goal, and that's to mine as well as you darn can.

To do that, you need to do three things: find resources, extract them, and return them to be stored in a safe area in as large amounts as is possible and as fast as is possible without dying.

To do that more often than you end up dead and far from your base, you need to keep a few things in mind.

The Camp

Perhaps the best habit you can adopt for yourself as a miner is to never mine far from a base. This doesn't mean you need to stay by your home, far from it. We just mean that if you're mining and there isn't a Chest or five, a Crafting Table, a Furnace, maybe a Bed and certainly some safe, safe walls to get to quickly, you're mining dangerously.

Mining free, with a base farther than a minute or so away, is a fine tactic when you're out exploring, just starting a world or otherwise unable to invest any large amount of time into the effort, but once you've established a home, you should rarely be mining without having a secure area nearby in which to resupply, deposit gathered resources and hide from the elements.

Camps can be built just about anywhere, as all you need to do is build a small room wherever you are. Don't hesitate to wall off a section of a cave or build a safehouse within a structure like a ravine, Fortress or any other. You have mastery over this land, if you'll take it, and you can never really have enough safehouses.

To produce the best results, plan your mines by first picking a good spot for a mining camp/ safehouse, such as at the bottom of a deep staircase, or built up in a natural structure such as a ravine or cave. Bring the stuff you'll need to build a good camp along with you to the spot you want to mine before actually mining, and it will make your ore collection progress much quicker than it otherwise would.

Well-lit tunnels are a must for any good camp.

Another shot of a good mining camp, complete with Chests, a Crafting Table and a furnace.

Camps can be as elaborate or simple as you'd like, but each should meet a few requirements: they should be secure from mobs (meaning they should be well-lit and only accessible through Doors or Trapdoors), they should be easily accessible from your mine (no more than a minute or two away from where you're mining), and they should contain a Chest with helpful items, a Crafting Table, a Furnace and possibly a Bed at the least.

Good items to bring to start a base include Wood of any kind (as well as Planks and Sticks), Cobblestone, tools and weapons, food, and Coal, Charcoal and Torches. Unless you expand your mining camps into more permanent bases, you should think of them as places to resupply and work temporarily, so transport rare or valuable items back to your main bases when you can.

This Miner has all the gear he needs to set out in search of ore.

Don't forget the armor and the Sword when you go minin'!

For Mining
3 or 4 Stone Pickaxes
2 or 3 Stone Shovels
At least 2 Pickaxes of higher quality
At least 1 Shovel of higher quality
1 full stack of Torches or more (4 stacks is a good number)
Enough food to get full from empty three times (cooked meat and Bread are great options)
1 full stack of Cobblestone, 2 at most (partially in order to make a Furnace)
Whatever Wood you can spare (a full stack of Wood is ideal, but at least some Wood, Wood Planks and/or Wood Sticks is a very good idea)

When First Setting Up Base Add
As many Torches as you can
As much Coal as you can
As much Wood as you can
3 more Shovels and Pickaxes of any type except Wood or Gold
2 or more Chests
1 Crafting Table
Some Iron Ore or Iron Ingots

The Gear

A Pickaxe is all you need to mine, but it's not the only item you should take with you on your trips. When you need to mine, plan an extensive mining excursion that takes a bit of time and gear, and your trips will be much more rewarding.

Miners out on a serious resource acquiring jaunt should take as much of the following kit as possible for best results. You might not be able to acquire all of this gear at first, so just take as much as you can and improve your kit as you expand. Eventually, you'll be able to add to this kit and outdo it by adding better items as you progress in your world.

Each time you go out on a planned trip to mine, take the mining kit with you, and stay out mining until you use it all up or run out of inventory space. By doing this and combining it with the practices below, you'll end up with the maximum number of resources in the least amount of time.

The Exploratory Trips

As tempting as it might be, don't go just randomly mining when you find a cave or other structure (or at least don't do so for long). Plan your trips, get your gear ready, know where your base is, and head out with an area in mind.

- The best mines are centered around a mineshaft (a vertical shaft with a ladder) or a staircase that goes from ground level to the bedrock. Build tunnels or clear out levels around these, never going too far from the center staircase or mineshaft and always going straight out from the center. No twisting passages or changing levels, just straight halls, rooms and tunnels with flat floors.
- Keep your mine organized, but also collect all resources you see. When you find ore, follow it and mine it all out, but when it's done, repair your mine so that you keep it easy to understand. For instance, if you come across some ore that goes below the level that the rest of your mine is on, mine it out and then replace the floor so that it stays flat.
- Remember the two rules of ore finding: ore is most common below level 16 and near Lava. If you're really looking for ore, you want to have a base in the lower levels so you can explore them, and you want to look out for Lava. When you find Lava, dig around it, containing it as you go, and you'll more than likely come across some nice resource deposits.

Best Mining Practices

Some general tips for mining, these will refine your tactics into well-developed, highly efficient processes.

- Use tools to breaking. You're already out, and though you might have some other project you feel like rushing off to, you're best served by using up the tools you have when you're already in your mine. If you take our mining kit with you and use it all up, you'll collect more resources each time you're out, making the time you spent in your mine much more worthwhile.
- Your mine should have a straight shot to the surface. We've covered this a bit before, but it bears reiteration, as it's so key to good mining. It should never be hard to get back to the surface from your mine, and if it is, you should make an easy exit for yourself.
- You should have a quick shot back to base when mining as well. Again, we've covered this but we're going to say it again: it should never take more than a minute or two to get back to a base from where you're mining. Keep mining far away from base and we can tell you from experience that a Creeper's gonna find you and ruin your day sooner than later.
- Deposit resources often. It's a guaranteed win when you take your resources back to your secure base no matter how little or how much you've gathered. Do it as much as possible.
- Leave no dark spots in your mines. No matter how small the shadowy spots are in your mine, light them up. You should never, ever have mobs spawning in the areas you are mining, and you can make that happen by using Torches and other light sources liberally.

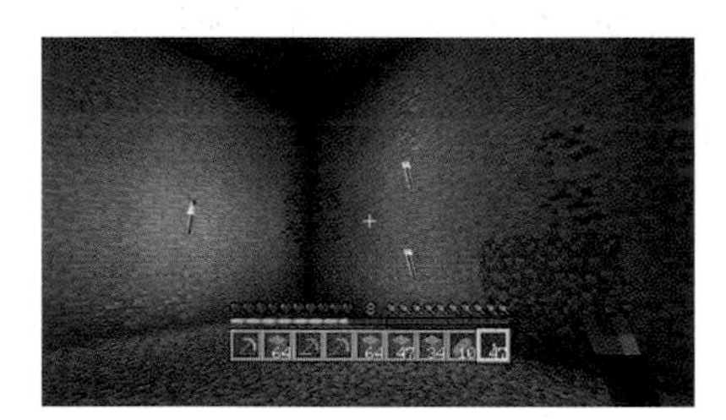

- Use signs to direct yourself. Whether it's telling you what level you're on or that a cave or base is "This Way," use signs. There's never going to be a moment where you are sad that a sign told you where something is, and there will be many times you wish there was one to help out.
- Keep your tools close together in your tray. Switching between tools like Pickaxes and Shovels can take up a lot of time over many switches, so keep them right next to each other and you'll save a lot of minutes.
- Go in pairs, with one player mining and the other organizing. If playing multiplayer, split the responsibilities by having one player expand the mine and gather resources while the other cleans up behind them and keeps the mine organized. It really is worth the trouble.
- Leave a third of your Iron tools by switching to Stone for mining lesser materials. Use your Iron tools on all materials until there's about a third of them left. Then switch to Stone tools unless you find something that requires Iron to break. This allows you to stay out longer, as you can still collect the more valuable ores while continuing to expand your mine.

The Bedrock Tunnel

This mining strategy technically belongs in the structures section, but as its purpose is almost exclusively related to mining, we've included it here.

In our mining (and even exploring) of the Minecraft world, few structures have come in as handy as The Bedrock Tunnel, which is exactly what it sounds like. By digging down to the Bedrock and building a well-organized cavern or tunnel, you are able to expand over large areas of the map easily, giving you access to the layers above. The terrain right above teh Bedrock level is almost always solid Stone and ore, with maybe a little Lava and Gravel, so you can usually count on being able to dig out a simple rectangular room or tunnel with ease.

This tunnel or room can then be expanded on (we've even seem some Crafters who dug out the entire bottom layer of the map, incredibly), and you can build mineshafts with Ladders up out of the Bedrock Tunnel to access the entire map above. This means that you can use your Bedrock Tunnel to test out various areas of the map for caves, ravines, Fortresses and other structures while having an easy area to return to (the Bedrock Tunnel) that contains safe-houses and eventually leads back to your main base. Add rails and Minecarts for even quicker access to the entire map.

Advanced Farming

Runnin' around and a'murderin' mobs in order to get food, or making maniacal runs on Villager Wheat farms, is all well and good, and will get you through the beginning of the game just fine. However, later in the game, having to leave your base for food trips can get exceedingly tedious and frustrating, and it usually leads to a cycle of taking quick hunting trips that never gather enough food, leading you have to go huntin' again not too far in the future.

In the end, having a ready food source built into your home such as a farm or ranch is almost a must for a Minecrafter, and they really aren't too hard to set up. Last Minecrafter we showed you a few neat and efficient ways to build some basic, high-yield farms and ranches that you can use to keep your food close and easy to get to, but despite making it a lot easier to acquire food than it would be by hunting, our farms and ranches still required you to do a bit of work when it comes to harvesting the food.

This being Minecraft, however, there is almost always a way to turn most tasks into automated systems that require very little input, and this is certainly the case with farms. If you want to step up your food acquisition game to the next level, give these builds a go.

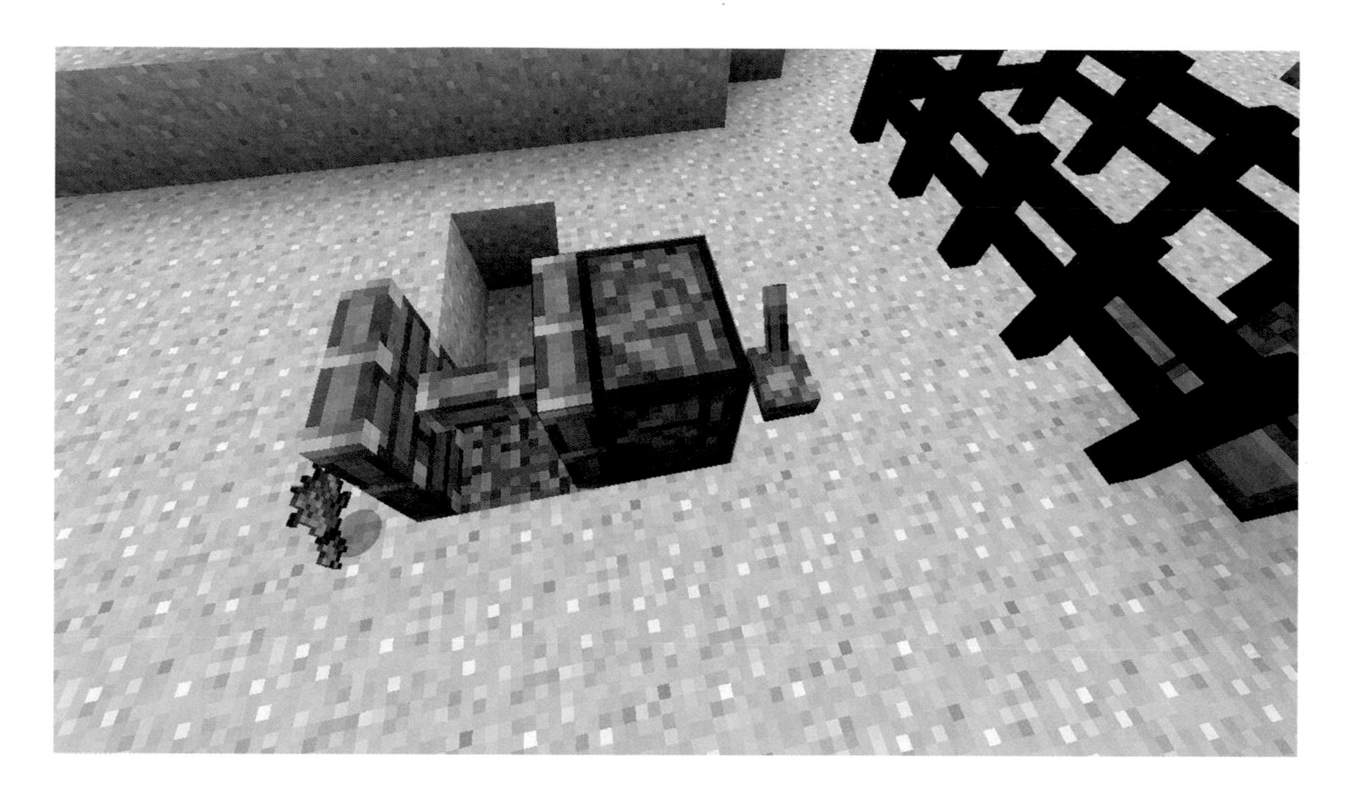

Two Styles of Automated Farms

Piston Farms can easily be attached to most existing farms.

The Piston Farmer

Pistons are one of the most dynamic and useful objects in the Minecraft universe, and when it comes to farming, they can help you out quite a lot. This build takes advantage of the fact that an activated Piston that shoves over a plot of grown Wheat will cause the Wheat to break and drop so you can grab it and use it.

This build can be added to most farms, but you'll need to leave at least one or two blocks next to each block where you will grow Wheat. All you need to do then is place a Piston on the empty block one block next to and one block above the block on which you're growing the Wheat. Make sure the Piston faces the Wheat, and do this for every block where there will be Wheat. Then, wire all of the Pistons together with Redstone so that they lead to one single Lever. (You may need some Repeaters.)

The Water Scythe caught in action as it harvests Wheat for you.

When you flip the Lever, all Pistons should extend across where the Wheat has grown, breaking the Wheat. Flip the Lever again so that the Pistons detract, and where there once was a Wheat farm, there is now a large amount of Wheat icons floating on empty patches of Dirt, and you can just run down your farm and grab them, replanting as you go.

The Water Scythe

Piston farming's fun, but when it comes to efficiency, nothing beats the Water Scythe. Like Pistons, Water that flows over a block of growing Wheat will break it. Unlike Pistons, however, flowing Water will actually carry the dropped Wheat with it.

By using both of these features, we can harvest an entire farm with the flick of a Lever and direct the flow of the Water so that all of the harvested Wheat gathers in one spot for you to pick up.

For this, you'll want to build your farm in a terrace formation, with one level of the farm one block below the other. Before you plant, go to the far end of the top level of your farm, and build a little wall with alcoves (holes) in it that line up with where the Wheat will be planted. Now, place Buckets of Water in the alcoves so that it flows out over the whole farmland, making sure that it doesn't overflow the sides. Test this out a bit so that you get it right.

Now move to the bottom level of your farm and see where the water is flowing out. Build around this so that all of the Water collects in one trench that goes downhill and ends in one single block (without overflowing).

Go back to the top of your farm and temporarily remove the Water. What you need to do now is control when the Water comes out. The best way to do this is by building a system of Sticky Pistons, blocks and a Lever, so that when you push the Lever, the Pistons remove the blocks from in front of the Water, allowing it to flow (and when you push it again, the Pistons put the blocks back and stop the Water). If you don't have or don't want to use Sticky Pistons, however, you can simply use a block of Dirt over the alcove that you punch out when you want to harvest your Wheat.

Once it's all set up, plant your Wheat and wait until harvest day, which will be the easiest one you've ever had.

Semi-Automated Breeding

An above view of the somewhat-workable Automated Breeding machine.

Unfortunately, the console version of the game is not yet set up to where we can have fully automated breeding, as there's no way to automate feeding animals Wheat yet, but you can set up a fun if not always well-functioning automated breeder using a few Powered Rails, Detector Rails and some Water.

Start your build with a pen for your selected animal. Make the pen lead to two Fence Gates that are separated by one block and that have a drop off immediately after them. You want your pen to funnel animals toward the Gates one at a time, and it's best if you can isolate two animals (one in front of each gate) if possible, so play around with Fences, Fence Gates, trenches and other methods to find the one that works best for you.

On the other side of each Gate (one block down from them), build a railway in this pattern: Powered Rail-Detector Rail-3 to 5 regular Rails-Detector Rail-Powered Rail. Make sure that there is a block at the end of the railway to stop the Minecart as well.

In the space between the two rails, dig a trench that starts one block deep and then one block before the end of the rails goes two blocks deep, and then three deep one block beyond that. Build a little pool at the end, and then dump a Bucket of Water at the top of the trench by the Gates so that it flows away from the pen and past the railways into the pool. Build a Fence immediately around your rails, blocking off the end so that animals can go under the Fence and into the pool, but never outside of the build.

The machine in action!

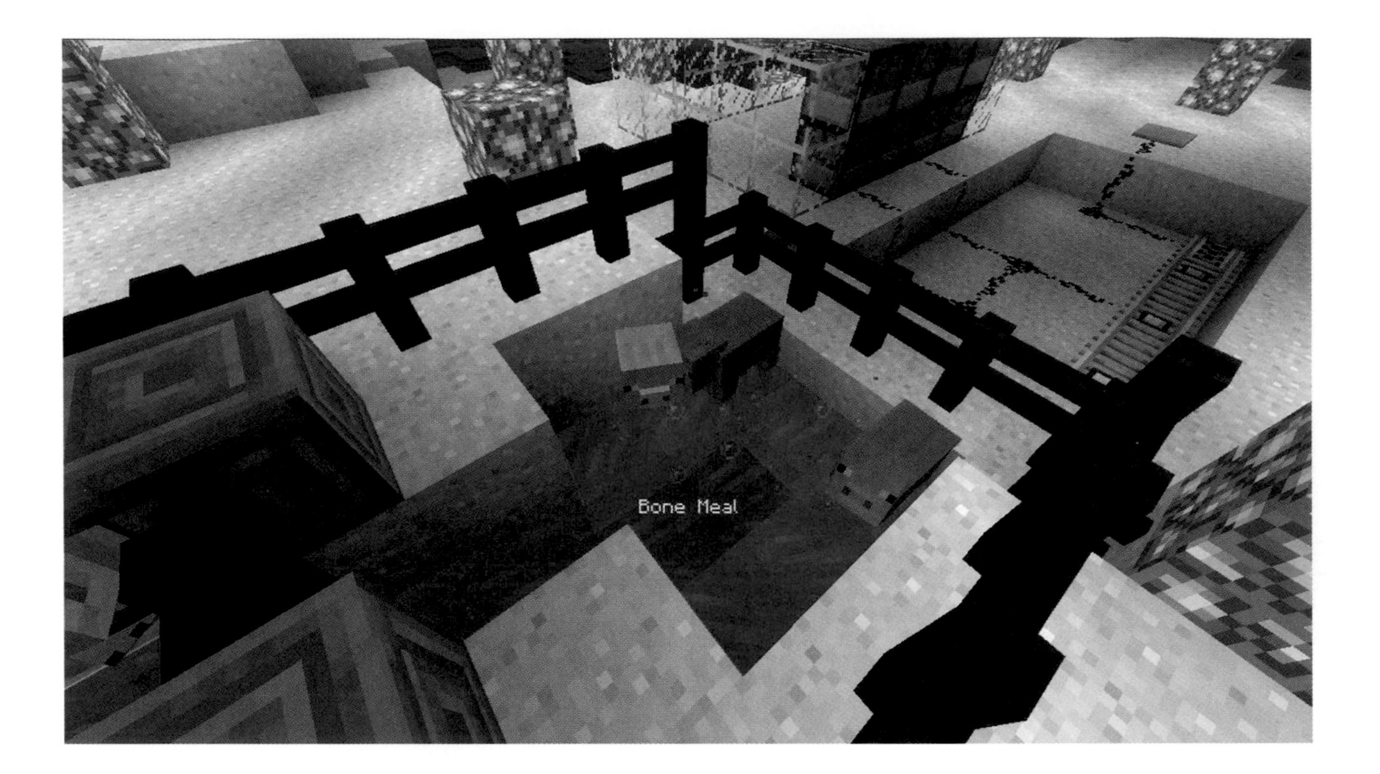

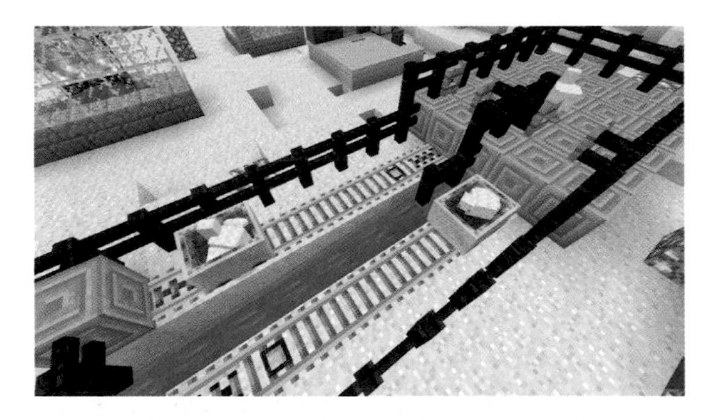

Note that these Pigs were brought down the canal and into the pen below, making them easy to harvest Pork from.

Finally, fill your pen with animals and set two Minecarts, one on each railway right in front of the fence. Use Wheat to put two animals into love mode (with the hearts above) and then open the Gates and lure them onto the carts.

What should happen if all goes well is that the animals in love will fall into the Minecarts, which will bounce down the track and then back again forever. As they pass each other, you should start to see baby animals pop up between them, which will hopefully fall into the Water and be pushed out into the pool.

Works for Chickens...and Cows too, as well as other breedable mobs (though it still can get messed up just as easily).

What can often happen, however, is that you will find it hard to get the mobs both in love mode and into the carts, and the baby mobs can often get in the way of the tracks meaning you need to give the carts a little push. You also tend to have to put animals back into love mode once they fall out, which can be hard to do while on carts.

It's not the best system, but it's pretty easy and fun to build, and as of right now, it's the best we've got for automated breeding. Tweak it here and there, such as maybe making there be a drop under the rails to where the water flows (so baby mobs simply have nowhere else to spawn), and you may be able to achieve better results. Hopefully in future they'll make this a little easier!

Building Advanced Structures

Now that you've been crafting a bit, you're probably ready to move beyond the basic house and want to sink your teeth into some serious builds. While the magic of Minecraft is that every person will find different ways to build their creations, we can help you in your quest to take your structures to the next level with these tips and ideas. Add your own touch to these, or use them in your own builds, and you'll find your world will soon be covered in unique architectural masterpieces.

Tips for Structure Pieces

Before we get to the big builds, here are some tips on incorporating commonly-used features into your structures. Most every build can be improved by a good staircase or window, and there's more to think about than just punching holes in walls for light or throwing down a stair or two.

Staircase

It's really, really easy to build a structure and then try and fit a staircase in it and fail miserably at making it look good and well-organized. This is because staircases need a certain amount of space, and we often build the main structure without making sure it has the necessary room for a staircase.

Remember this when making a staircase: the smallest workable staircase goes up at least two blocks and out at least three while being at least two blocks wide. This staircase is the bare minimum, and you have to remove the blocks you use to build the actual stair pieces on after you place them in order to have enough room to use the staircase.

Keep this in mind as you're building, and test your area as you go using blocks of Dirt in place of where your stairs will be. If you use Dirt blocks to see how and if a staircase will fit in your new build when you've only built one or two levels of it, you'll be able to make any adjustments to the floor plan before you build much. This can save a lot of time and effort, as it's often the case that a large section of a building has to be removed and tweaked in order to fit in a good staircase.

Another method is to build your staircases attached to the main building in their own little tower that's outside the rest (think parking garage staircases). This doesn't always fit with a build, but it can give you lots of room inside the main structure and add an aesthetic flair to your build if done well.

One final thought is to build the staircase around the entire outside of your building. This looks very cool on towers and is best for structures that are taller than they are wide, but it can also be a little dangerous if you don't add some Fences as railing.

Villager houses show an easy way to make a flat-ended pyramid roof with stairs.

Another pyramid-style design for a roof.

Roofs

Roofs are, for the most part, pretty easy to make, but we have just three thingswe wanted to mention that we think will improve your roof-building game.

Don't feel confined to flat roofs. Most builders start off their first few structures as just square buildings with flat roofs, and these are fine, but try out a pyramid-style roof. They're very easy and have an attractive look about them, and they separate your houses from those of a newby.

Use Stairs to give roofs a different texture. Stairs are kind-of the unofficial shingles of the Minecraft world, and using them on your roof will break up the monotony of blocky roofs.

Consider giving the roof a lip. Whether flat, terraced or otherwise built (we've seen some

Use different colored blocks in patterns on roofs for neat symmetrical effects.

awesome domes, which we'll talk about below!), think about giving the edge of your roof a lip, meaning it sticks out at least a block over the wall of the structure below. Besides looking good, this actually has a very practical reason: it keeps Spiders from being able to climb to the top of your home. Spiders can only go up straight walls or inclines, but can't make it over a lip. If you keep finding those pesky pixelated arachnids on top of your house, you might want to give this a go.

Domes are just awesome-looking, and can also provide protection from mobs while allowing sunlight in!

These windows are low, so using Glass is the best idea.

Windows

Of all these structures, windows are the ones where you're probably going, "Hey, I can build a window, man." Well, that's probably true, we can all punch a hole in a wall and let the light in, but can you build a good window? Here are some tips to help you, some of which are common sense and some that you might not have thought of yet.

Never just leave an empty space as a window unless you're very high up. This is something that we all do, but shouldn't, and those who continue to do so will find out why eventually when a Skeleton shoots through, a Creeper blows up or a Spider sneaks in. Always cover up your window with something at lower levels, unless you're absolutely sure nothing will be able to see in and try and attack you. Annoying darn Skeletons.

Use Glass or Glass panes at lower levels, never Fences, except for one-block wide murder holes. Place murder holes (one-block windows with a fence in them) in areas where there's plenty of room to move around, and use them by peeking out and shooting arrows through at the mobs beyond, then ducking away if needed (such as when fighting those pesky Skeletons).

A solid row of Fence windows going all the way around a building will keep Spiders from climbing up to your roof. Spiders can't crawl over Fences (nothin' can!), so using them at the top of a build all the way around it will effectively remove the Spider threat from your roof.

Windows don't have to only go in buildings!

Build little pool areas for the Elevator to deposit into (to avoid spills)

Water Elevator

They're not exactly the most realistic architectural feature you're going to have in your house, but when you need to go up and down a long way quickly and without having to spend a lot of resources or time building a Ladder or Stairs, you want a Water Elevator. Building one is about as easy as it gets: find a place where you want to be able to go from high to low (or vice versa) quickly, and drop a Bucket of Water so that it flows over the side of your high spot and down below. You'll want to build a little pool for the Water to catch in, and placing the Bucket of Water in a little controlled cubby at the top of the elevator can help keep it contained to one block (you usually only want them one block wide, bigger gets complicated).

This hole of Water looks unassuming, but it's actually an elevator that goes all the way to the Bedrock.

These tried-and-true, well-used structures are awesome for getting to and from deep mines or high castles, though you do need to make sure that the elevator is not too long, as you will have to breathe at some point. Most Crafters have at least one or two of these around their map, and you just have to try one out to see how useful they are.

Note: Some Crafters make small one or two block wide pools on the surface that look like plain water ponds, but when you dive in, they actually take you down to a secret base! Of course, if someone falls in or sees you dive in and not come back out, you might have an uninvited guest sooner rather than later.

Some Crafters have experimented with different shapes and styles to create fancier Elevators, some of which utilize Boats.

Structures

And now for the real meat: the big structure ideas. Use these as a jumping-off point for your own builds, or try one out when you're bored and looking for a new project. More than likely, you'll find something to add or make your own with these, and that's what Minecraft is all about, young Crafter.

Start your tower by shaping it out on the ground with Dirt first.

Towers Done Right

Nothing says "accomplished Crafter with awesome buildin' skills" like a big darn tower shooting up off of a mountain-top, and they're often one of the first advanced structures that Crafters build after their initial house.

The primary thing to keep in mind when building a tower is that you should plan out the build a bit before you get going. Take a look at our tips on staircases above, and make sure before you build too much that you know how you are going to incorporate a way to get up and down your new tower. Staircase? Ladder? Water elevator? They all work, but they all require a little planning to do well.

Also, think about whether you want the tower to just look cool or whether it should have room to do things in. You have to build your tower's base pretty large to accommodate both a staircase and rooms to do things in, so keep that in mind when planning. One good trick is to make most of the bottom part of the tower the housing for a grand staircase which goes up to a single floor and ends. Build more floors above that floor, but use a series of Ladders to get between these top floors instead of a staircase. This allows you to have a neat staircase (always prettier than just a Ladder), a tall tower and some rooms to put things in.

Another idea to consider is to make your entire tower a useful, functioning piece of your world by making it into a lighthouse. Adding a bunch of Torches or Glowstone to your tower at the top will allow it to be seen from quite far away (if there's nothing tall in the way, like a mountain or Jungle Biome), which is very helpful when navigating the wild. Not only does it tell you where home is, it gives you a constant focus point, which does wonders for learning the land around your base.

The inside of a completed tower.

At some point in your Pit, build a little base so that you don't have to go all the way up to your main base constantly.

The Great Pit

When it comes to easy-to-navigate mining structures that allow for excellent ore-finding and also look really cool, the Giant Pit is one of the best. Essentially just a big hole all the way down to the Bedrock, these work great when you start one a few levels beneath your base and, and they can add a dramatic flair to your home (while also providing a huge number of resources).

Construction of these is deceptively simple: all you need to do is dig down in a predetermined shape (usually just a square). However, if you've never undertaken removing this much material from one area, it can take a lot longer than you'd expect. The best method we've found is to cut out the border of the shape you'd want, and then walk along it row by row pointing down and mining out as many blocks as you can reach. Stand on the row behind the one you're mining, and then move back one row after you mine the whole row in front of you out.

For greatest efficiency, leave any ore you uncover that's outside of your shape alone for now and go back to them later, using them as reference points to start horizontal mineshafts off of your pit. You should also build a staircase along the edge of your pit as you work and add a one-block thick column up the center that goes back to your base by means of a Ladder. Use the staircases to move around the outside and work on various levels, while the Ladder in the center is for easy entrance and exit from the pit. Of course, this project is going to move along much quicker if mining together with a friend.

Like towers, Pits work best when drawn out beforehand.

Once done, put a little base at the bottom of the pit, and you'll have quick access to every level, not to mention having uncovered quite a bit of ore and possibly even some structures.

Note: If you crack into a ravine, Fortress or other structure, continue the shape of your pit by walling it off from the structure you've cracked into. Mark where the structure is, or better yet use Glass as the walls, and you'll be able to access it easily and much more safely than you normally would (another bonus of the Great Pit).

A completed Water base from the outside.

The Underwater Base

Who doesn't want to live underwater, right? In Minecraft this is totally possible, but it does take some planning. If you swim down and try to just build some walls and put a roof on it, you're going to notice that your house is sort-of totally filled up with Water, which isn't exactly easy to live in. Plus it lets Squids in your home, which is just weird.

In order to build a base that won't drown you, you need to build the shape of the structure you want and then mine out the middle of it. Do this by making the shape of the building you want with blocks (fill the whole thing in as you go, don't leave any part hollow). Once you've got the shape of the building completed, put a Door down right in front of where you want the actual Door to be (so one block in front of your structure on the ocean floor). Doors are one of a few items that when placed cause Water to repel away from them, so you can then open the Door and punch out the two blocks behind it (in the shape of the Door) without flooding the space they leave with Water.

Once you've started into your base, hollow out the rest of it, making sure to plug up any holes you create quickly before the Water can flow in and fill the base. Once you've got it hollowed out, you can start adding things to it like you normally would to a base, and you can even make windows if you're quick enough to drop a block in quickly.

The primary problem, of course, with building underwater bases is staying underwater long enough to build without drowning. In order to do this, use the trick where Water will not flow through certain blocks that you can then move to. Ladders, Doors and Fences all leave at least some space around them that you can stick your head into and breathe, but Water does not enter the blocks they are on, meaning you can build little underwater breathing areas with these items.

Crafter Darkscour took the underwater base to a whole 'nother level with this one.

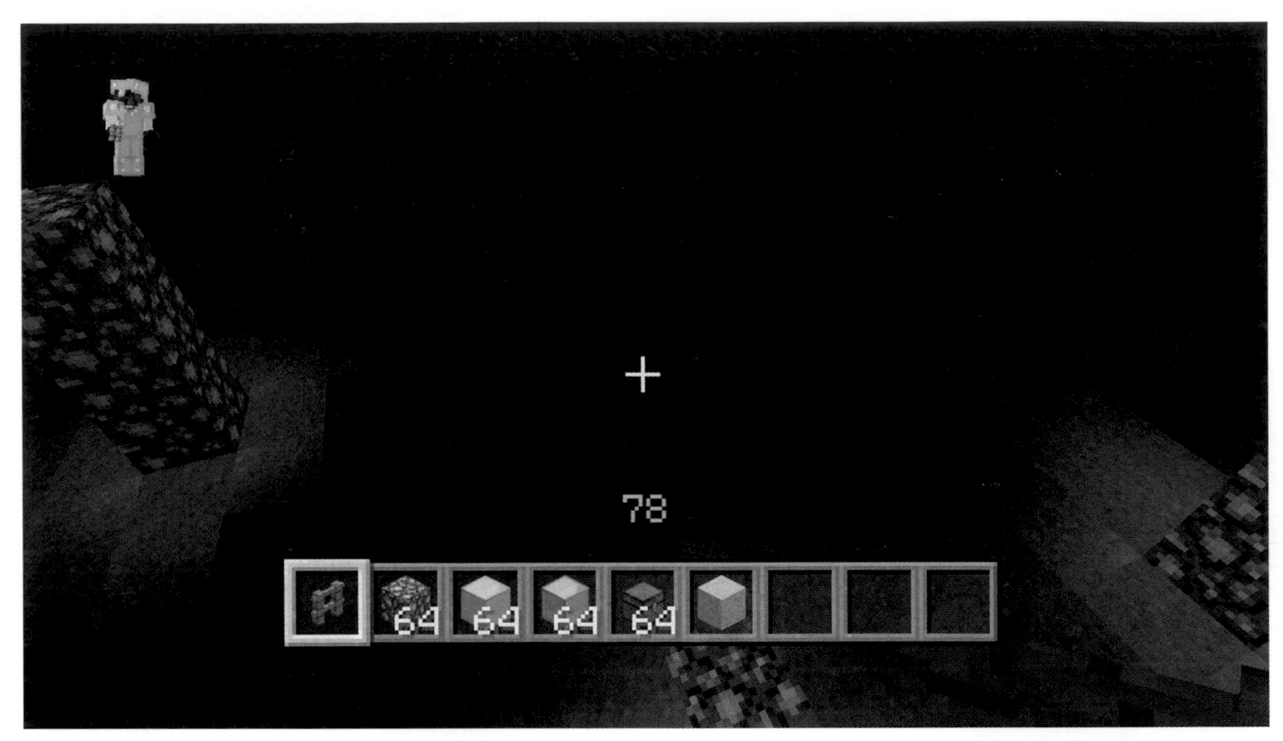

Dropping a shell like this one from above helps you avoid having to be underwater without air for as long.

Use an outline like this one to make it easier to drop your Sand or Gravel.

Another method is to use gravity-influenced blocks like Sand or Gravel to build the shape of your structure from above, dropping them down so they fall through the Water and down to where you want them. You'll still have to swim down and put down a door, and you'll need to replace the outer layer with something solid like Stone (or surround the whole thing and just mine out the Sand), but this method can make your planning go much quicker overall.

The Double Bluff Base

Getting robbed or having your home damaged by other players online is less common on the console than on the PC version, but attacks like this (called "griefing") do happen. It has become common practice in PVP (or just busy) servers for players to go to some lengths to hide their bases and loot, whether through putting them in obscure locations, building complex traps and other deterrents or (our favorite method) through tricks such as fake bases.

Of the many styles of fake base we've seen, none is so effective as the awesome and fun-to-build Double Bluff Base. The premise is simple: build a fake base that is actually an entrance to your real base. This method is highly effective for two reasons: 1) Players looking for your base will get excited, and then quickly disappointed and bored when they realize it's a "fake" base. Few will ever come back, and if they mess it up or take stuff, it doesn't matter because it will mostly be filled with cheap stuff. And 2) You can move in and out of this area without people wondering what's up, as they'll think you're just improving your fake base.

A small house like this against a hill and covered by Trees is a perfect fake base.

The fake base works by building a small structure that has a method for opening an entrance to a larger one that is hidden behind or underneath the smaller "fake" base. The three main components of making this build successful are:

- Making the fake base detailed enough to trick people
- Hiding the larger structure as well as possible
- Building an entrance to the real base that is hard to notice and to open

When it comes to the fake base, what you want is to imagine what would draw you in if you thought you were close to another player's real base, and then what would frustrate you and make you leave. So, for instance, you don't want the fake base to be too easy to find (so don't put giant glowing towers or the like), but you don't want to entirely hide it either. Make it so that there's one direction that part of it can be pretty easily seen from or

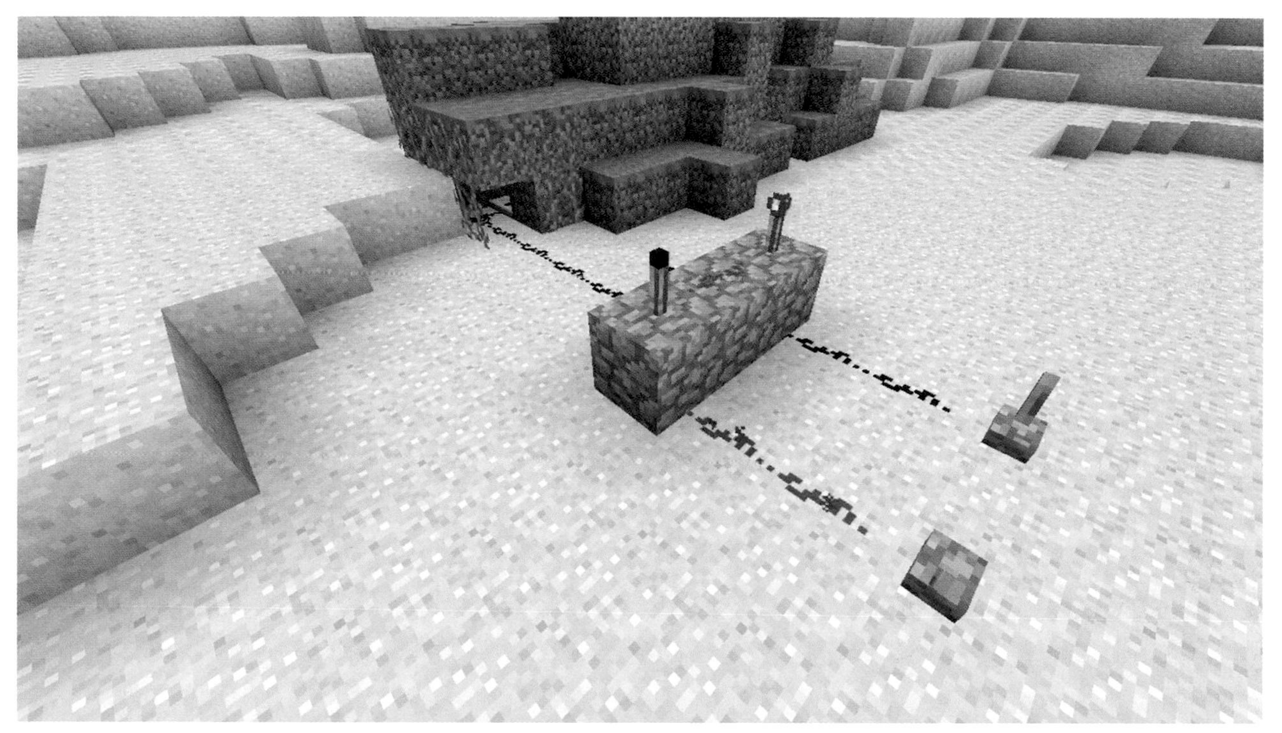

An example AND Gate hooked up to our secret door in this false hill. Of course, for yours you want to put your switches farther away from each other and hide all of the Redstone underground.

something similar. Inside, you want it to look real when a player approaches (so looks real from the outside, can see things like a few Chests, etc. inside it from the outside), but when a player actually enters, it shouldn't take them long to realize it's fake, as there shouldn't be much more inside.

Make this bluff even more effective by adding a few simple traps (like Pressure Plates attached to Arrow shooting Dispensers) and maybe even some signage that indicates the base is fake ("Haha, got you sucker!" or that kind of thing). For the fake loot Chests, fill them with something annoying like Gravel, and your intruders should take off pretty quickly.

Your real base should be in a mountain or hill directly behind the fake one, or buried underneath it. Remember: this is your secret base, so keeping it completely hidden and as safe as possible is paramount (don't go adding windows or easy-to-see Doors or the like on the outside). Make it so that if a player were to walk by or over it, they wouldn't notice anything different from a normal area and will think that there is just natural landscape around them.

One good idea is to put at least four or five layers of block between your base and your fake base by creating a tunnel or hallway after the secret door. Invaders of your fake base will often punch out the ground to see if there's anything below, so trick them further by making it seem like there isn't.

A view of the Sticky Pistons that drive the secret door.

Another trick for keeping your base safe and concealed is to build an outer shell (around your base but still underground or inside a mountain so it can't be seen) of Obsidian or Lava. That way if a player does dig down and hit your base, all they see is a wall of tough-to-get-through Obsidian or Lava. Usually, they'll just turn back, and if they don't, they will probably have a very hard time getting in.

The final touch, and the most important for your secret base is, of course, your secret door. There are many, many methods and strategies for doing this, and you can come up with your own if you like, but ours involves using an AND Gate (see the Advanced Inventions section) with two hidden Levers that, when flipped at the same time, cause two Sticky Pistons attached to two blocks to slide back, revealing the door to your true base.

Build the secret door into your floor or a wall, attaching blocks of the surrounding natural material (Stone or Dirt usually) that is in the area. Hide your Sticky Pistons and Redstone behind more blocks of the same material or underground, and run the Redstone through a hidden AND Gate (you'll probably need some Repeaters to stretch the signal), and then to two Levers. Place one Lever in your fake base (have it function to do something else as well, like open a Door, for another layer of trickery) and one Lever someplace else, preferably out of sight and well-hidden. This way someone can come in and flip the Lever in your base and not open the secret door unless you have already flipped the second Lever, making your base secure.

Building into Natural Structures

This is less of a specific build and more of a fun concept: why not let nature do the design for you and just build into a mountain or cliff-side? Minecraft's environment-constructing algorithms are pretty awesome at times, as anyone who has come around a corner and gone "Whoa" when they saw what was there knows. Make that "natural" beauty your own and incorporate a home into it. Having to work within and around the shape that's already there, and building by removing blocks instead of adding (for the most part), can spark the imagination and get a builder thinking differently, and it makes for some neat builds.

View of a lake from a cliff? We say yes to that.

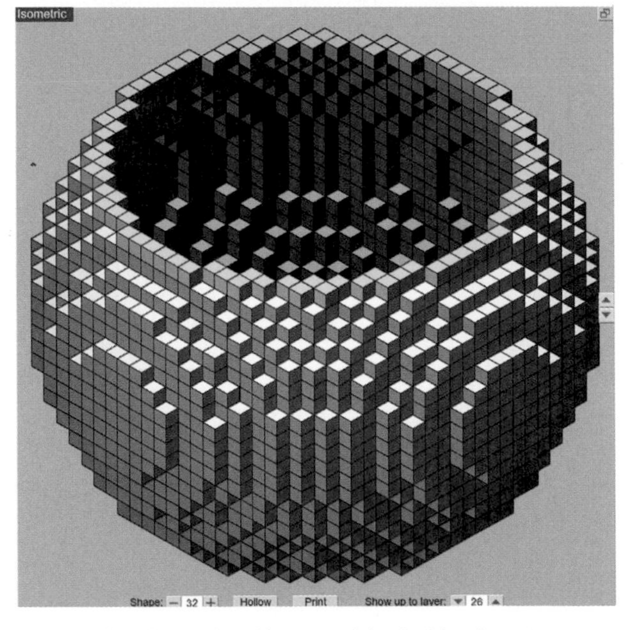

This is what the tool at Plotz.co.uk looks like showing you how to build a layer of a sphere.

Structure Tools

Planning out big structures can be hard, and planning out giant, symmetrical structures like domes? Well that takes a seriously organized mind to get right without help. Lucky for us non-math geniuses, there are actually some really cool tools online to help you plan out your build, and they're free!

There are basically two types of main tools out there right now: plotting tools that allow you to draw out plans for a whole build, and math-based tools that show you layer-by-layer how to build complex structures like orbs and domes.

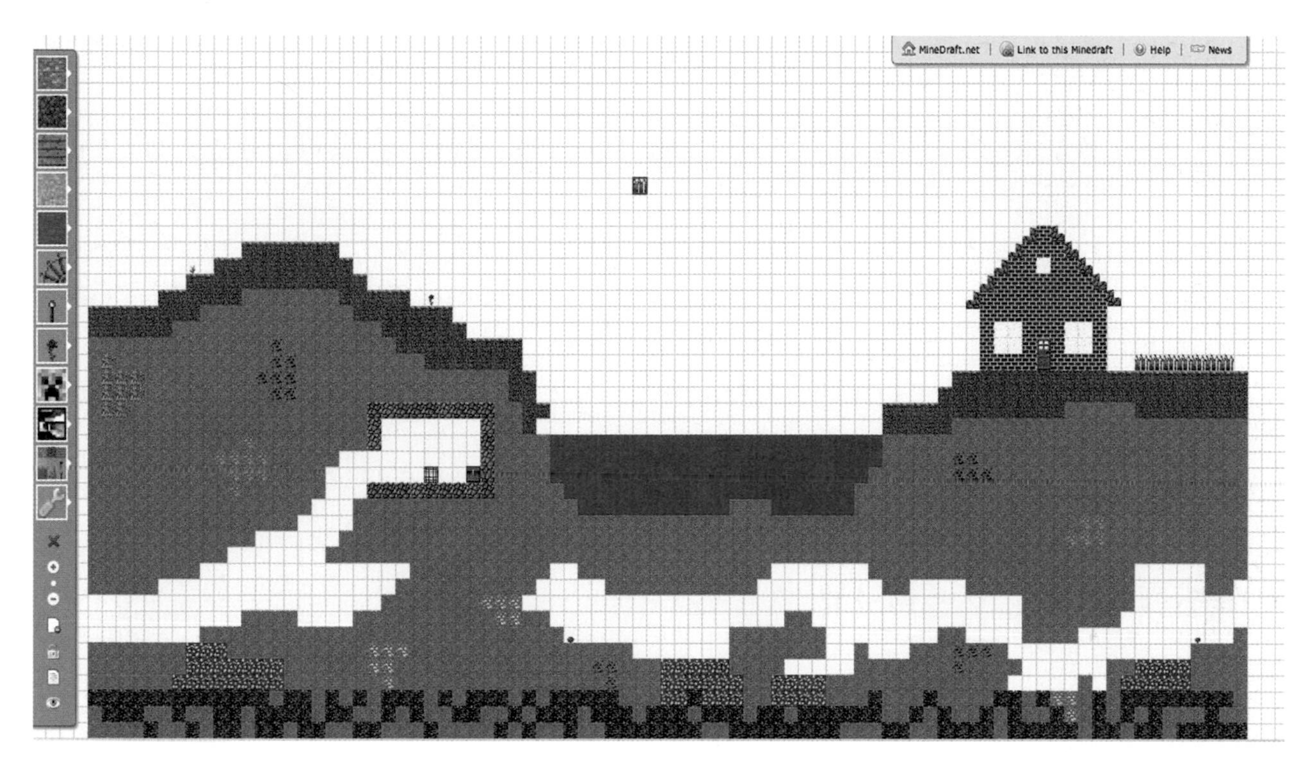

MineDraft lets you plan out your builds vertically or horizontally.

In the first category, check out **MineDraft.net.** This straightforward site simply gives you a grid on which to place representations of the various blocks and items in the game. Click on the block you'd like, put it where you want on the grid, and continue until you've got a map of your next build. Especially great for working out Redstone circuits, this tool is a tremendous help for complex builds.

For the more math-based tools, Plotz.co.uk is king of the spheres. What we mean by that is that it's a site that helps you build spheres and domes of various sizes by showing you what to build layer by layer. Instead of having to keep the entire, giant dome in mind while counting the blocks, so it ends up even and nice-looking, Plotz does it for you, and you simply have to recreate what you see on the screen. Your domes will never look so crisp and perfect!

Plotz also shows you how to build a few random structures, like this observatory.

What To Do When

There's a moment in just about every long-haul Crafting session where you come up against something tough, and you're just not sure what to do about it. Minecraft is full of these kind of moments, whether it's deciding to stay down in your mine for another fifteen minutes before heading back to base, or whether you suddenly find yourself in peril and aren't sure if you should fight, fly or just throw in the towel and reload from your last save. While there are really no wrong answers in this game that's all about experimentation and playing how you like, there are some tips for certain situations that we can give you that can make your next mining trip go a bit smoother (by which we mean less full of death and woe).

1. You're lost and can't find home (or anything else you recognize).

We all love the goofy, blocky graphics of Minecraft, but we also have to admit that they can make it hard to keep your sense of direction. Since there are only so many types of blocks and environments, you can quickly get turned around both above and below ground. If you're stuck out in the wild and are starting to think you'll never see home again, try these tips.

- Get up high. If you're above ground, create a dirt tower so you can look out over a bigger area, or climb a tree. If you're underground, stop trying to find your way out naturally and just dig up in a staircase pattern. Moving up is almost always beneficial in Minecraft when lost or stuck, and you can always go back down if you need to!
- Mark your path. Always, always mark your path, especially when you're already lost. Use towers, torches, just about anything you'll recognize, and you'll start to weed out all the wrong directions (and will stop going in circles, as can definitely happen).
- Use the Cobblestone/Nether Rack "north" trick. If you look at blocks of either of these, you'll see that they have an "L" shape on the texture (on the regular texture pack). If you situate your miner so that the L is facing the correct direction (meaning it looks like the letter should), you are facing north.

2. You're stuck outside/underground without resources and mobs are about.

Mobs don't care if you're ready for combat or not: they're coming for you. It's pretty likely that you're gonna find yourself in a bad spot at some point, with mobs a'comin' and no Sword, Bow or other weapons to speak of. What do you do?

- Get up high. Like with being lost, getting off the ground level is an excellent combat measure. Mobs have a hard time climbing even one block and most cant climb two (just Spiders), so put some air between you and your foes.
- Run straight through. Sometimes the best way to survive is to just put on a burst of speed and try and break through the line of mobs. If possible, eat something before you do this.
- Protect your resources. It's always easier to come back and find a Chest with items in it than it is to rush back to get the gear that dropped when you died. Bring Chests with you when you mine and store all of your important stuff when in a bad spot before trying to escape.
- If possible, build a mini-mini murder fort. Obviously you don't have time to do any major construction, but if you can surround yourself with blocks and leave just a little space to attack through, you should be able to time it so that you can hit mobs and they can't reach you. Very effective in a pinch.

3. There's a Creeper in your home (or project, or mine, etc.).

It happens, sometimes a lot, and it's terrifying. There's one thing to do.

- Get out. Immediately. It's the Creeper's home now. Okay, not really to that last bit, but seriously, just go. While you might be able to kill the thing, there's just too much at risk. Unless you don't care what happens to the place, it's always better to leave and let the creepy thing see itself out or despawn than it is to risk having to put half your house back together.

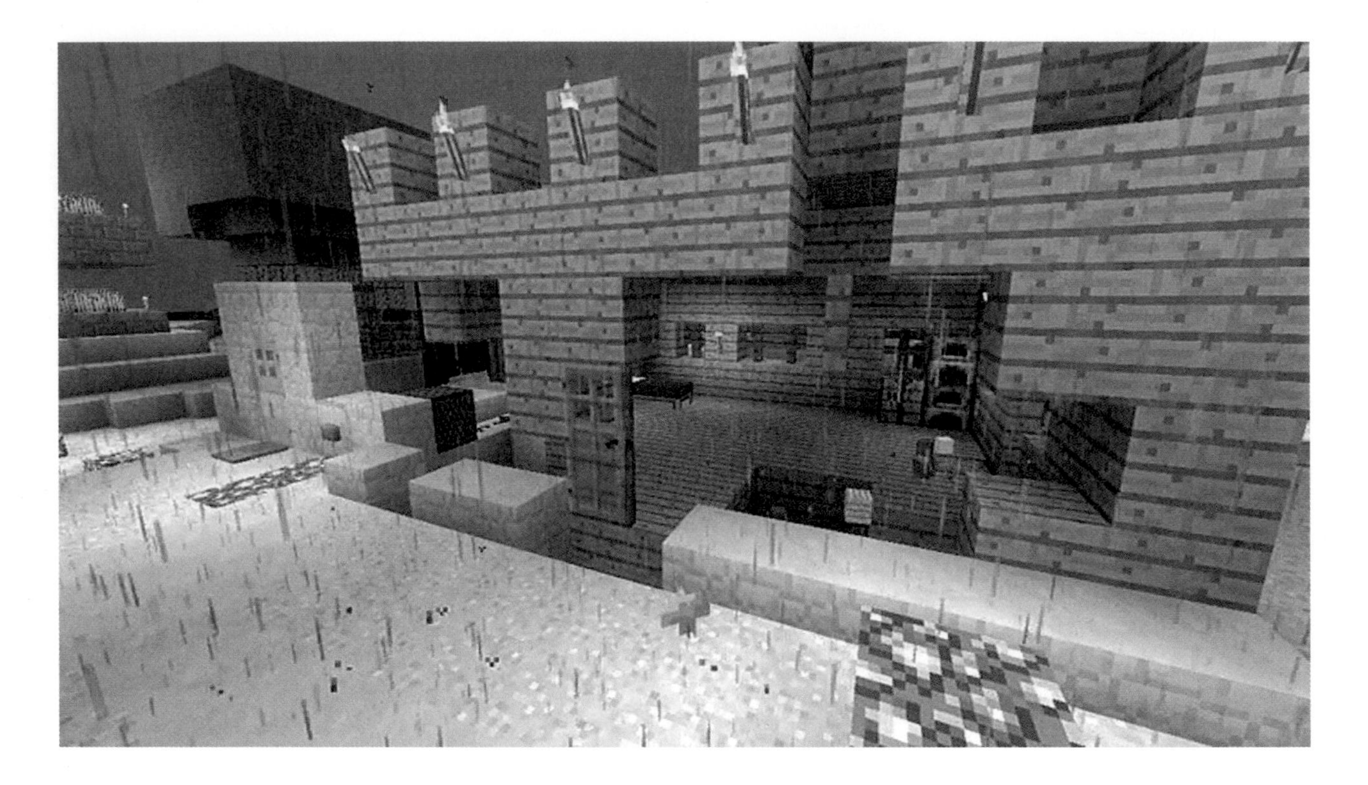

4. A Creeper done blew up your home.

But of course, sometimes you just can't get away in time. Creepers do be creepin'. But don't panic; you have options.

- Consider reloading. It may seem cheap, but so is showing up unannounced, sneaking right next to you and your beloved project and blowing it to smithereens. If you saved less than five minutes ago or if rebuilding would take more time than re-doing what you've been doing, you might want to reload.
- Take the opportunity to make it better. We all get distracted by new projects and tend to leave old ones sitting for a long time. It's super common to jump in someone's world and see that their bedroom is a lot shabbier than whatever the newest project they're workin' on is, as miners often get so caught up in other stuff that they don't take the time to update or upgrade their older work. If a Creeper knocks a hole in your house, well maybe it's time to add that moat you've always wanted! This is one of the greatest things about Minecraft: when things get destroyed, it gives you the chance to make it better!

5. You fell in a pit/cave/ravine without torches.

Falling into darkness is hard and a bit nerve-wracking; it usually starts with a bit of panic as you wonder how you can possibly get out without light. But...

- Just dig forward and up. Hopefully you have tools, but either way, just put a block in front of you (you can always kinda just a bit, even in the dark) and break it. Then point up and break the one above it, and then the one behind that. Jump up and repeat. You will eventually either A) find light, B) get out or C) crack into another drop and fall more, possibly to your death. Whatever happens, you'll at least get out.

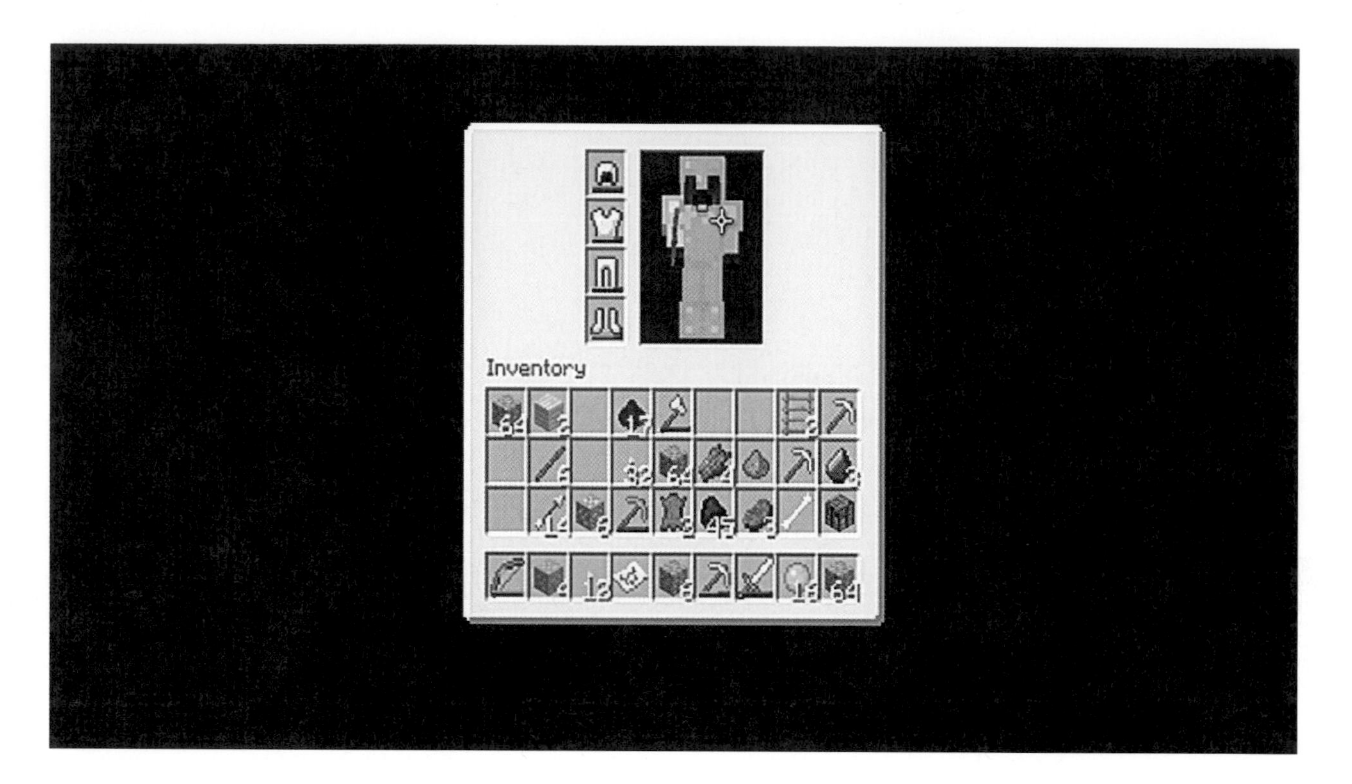

6. You have a bunch of resources and wonder if it's time to go back, but aren't sure if you want to yet.

Oh the many, many times we've thought to ourselves "I should find a Chest, but I'll just explore this one more cave." There's an answer:

- Don't stay out. If you're wondering if you should head to a Chest, the answer is almost always yes. Think of it like this: you just did a bunch of work, you have some good stuff, and you are currently safe, healthy and you know the way back. These are things you know for sure, right now. Give Minecraft the chance, and it will change one or all of those things within seconds. Err on the side of caution (and keeping your loot).
- Or, build a chest here and now and drop yer goods. You can always come back in a few minutes and grab it all, and at least you know it'll be safe.
- Or, save the game. Don't be afraid to use the save feature to your advantage. Hit pause and save real quick, that way you can load from right there and make a better decision if things go south.

7. You find somethin' awesome, but you aren't geared/prepared/ready to jump into it.

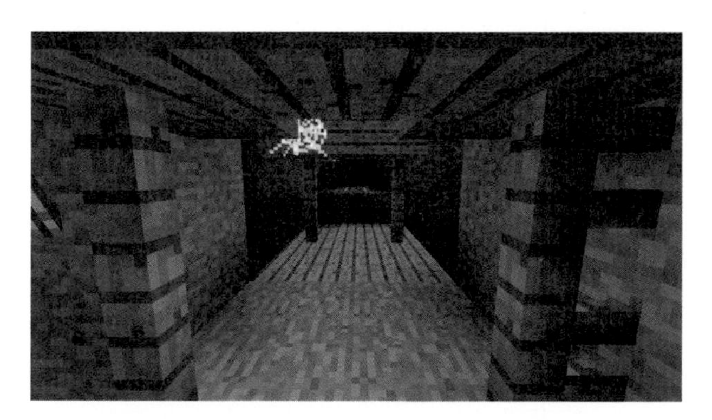

Abandoned Mineshafts are one of the more dangerous structures in the game. Don't go in unless you're ready.

Cool things are around almost every corner, and you'll end up stumbling across a ton of them while you were on your way elsewhere.

- Don't overreach. Taking a peek is fine, but if you don't think you're prepped for a big cave encounter, **don't go down the big, dark, dangerous cave.**
- Mark it well. Light the place up with Torches, build a big tower of Dirt, make a Flower path back home or better yet bust out a Map and write down the coordinates. Just because you aren't ready to go now doesn't mean you should let neat places and valuable areas be forgotten. Make it so you'll definitely be able to find it again, and then do.

8. A structure or area is giving you trouble because it is getting too complex and dangerous.

In most games, you're pretty much stuck with having to navigate complex areas as they are, but this is Minecraft. We have better ways of dealing with nests of enemies, such as...

- Take the area apart. Just start simplifying the area by removing blocks and making it into one big room. You don't have to play fair; mobs certainly don't. Turn that confusing cave system or dangerous mineshaft into *your* area. Eliminate the threat by controlling the land, and you'll find that Fortresses and the like are just oh so much less intimidating.

9. Something interesting pops up while you're in the middle of a project.

Say you're carving out a base, and you stumble across the entrance to a cave or a big deposit of ore. What do you do? Abandon your project and deal with this now, or save it for later?

- If it's ore, go for it. Get ore until there is no more, and then fill in the area so it is just Cobblestone. Your later projects will thank you, and you won't lose the organization of what you were working on.
- If it's a structure or system, secure the area, mark it, and come back later. There is nothing more dangerous than leaving an entrance to an open cave or structure in your base or project, because you never know what can come sneaking up out of the depths all the way through your home and even to your bedroom. Where there's dark, there's danger. Control the situation first, finish what you were working on, then come back and dominate that structure and whatever foolish mobs dare to dwell in it.

10. You can't find what you're looking for.

Sometimes you start a game and crack straight into a Diamond-filled ravine/Fortress, and sometimes you go weeks on a world without seeing either. While it's never guaranteed to find anything in the game, there is a system that can help.

- Use the Staircase Down, Ladder Up method. Seriously guys, this method works wonders. All you do is create a staircase down to the Bedrock and when you're at the bottom, build a Ladder that goes all the way to the surface from there. Create a few of these in different directions and on different parts of the map, and you end up covering an enormous area in very efficient manner. You'll find ore, you'll find structures, you'll find mobs; you'll find just about everything. Even more effective when combined with tunnels, branch mining and clearing out levels around the staircase.

Beating the Game

Where You Should Be in Your Game

Most games of Minecraft that actually reach The End happen one of two ways: either the players collect the needed items as they otherwise play and get the opportunity naturally (which takes a very long time), or they specifically set out at some point to collect what they need to get to The End and make it a goal. It really isn't likely that you can play casually and even get to The End, and even if you do, you are even less likely to do well there, as it is arguably the toughest scenario in the entire game.

You'll need the best gear you can get to beat Minecraft.

Because of this, your game should be fairly well along before you attempt The End. Check off as many items as possible from the following list before you make your trip, and your chances at success will multiply.

You Need

- Diamond gear (as much as possible)
- Lots of Obsidian (meaning more Diamonds needed in order to make Pickaxes)
- The ability to enchant (requires Diamonds, Obsidian and a Book to make an Enchantment Table)
- Potions (requires a Blaze Rod for a Brewing Stand)

As Diamonds are the hardest ore to find in the game, and two of the other three items on this list require Diamond (and the last a Blaze Rod, even harder to find), you'll need to either set out to find Diamonds early in the game, or be at a point where you've collected quite a bit already before you can think about going to The End.

Ye Olde Nether Portal, ready to go.

Part 1: Getting to the Nether

One of the primary ingredients for getting to The End is the Blaze Rod, which drops when Blazes are killed in the Nether. Naturally then, getting to the Nether is your first goal, and of course, this means you need a Nether Portal.

There are two ways to create a Nether Portal: either mine Obsidian and create the Nether Portal shape (Obsidian surrounding an empty space that's two blocks wide and three tall), or use Water poured over Lava that is in the correct shape to create the Portal. The first method takes Diamond, but a lot less finagling with Lava, while the second lets you skip the Diamond. We suggest going the longer, Diamond-using route however, as the benefits of collecting a lot of Diamond will help you out later.

Nether Forts can look like this when they spawn over Lava. Look for bridges and towers.

Part 2: The Nether

Once in the Nether, you need to create a safe area that you can base out of. Though you can't place Beds in the Nether (they will simply explode), you can bring building materials. Cobblestone is resistant to Ghast explosions, as is Obsidian, so using one or both of those materials to create a little base is an excellent idea. It's also prudent to take decent armor and weapons along, at the very least bringing some Iron gear if you can't go all the way for Diamond.

When you're set up with a safe place, you need to start looking around for Nether Forts. This can be a bit tricky, as your spawn point in the Nether can often be underground, requiring you to dig a while. However, if you find a pretty big room, especially one with a giant Lava pool at the bottom, you've probably found an area with a Nether Fort in it. The Nether is much smaller than the overworld, so if you don't see a Fort close around your base, you should try digging straight, skinny tunnels until you find one. Another option is to create a second Nether Portal in the overworld in a different spot, as this will spawn you elsewhere in the Nether.

The Blaze spawner in action, plus a random Magma Cube.

When you find a Nether Fort, look for Blaze spawners. These are usually on little Nether Brick platforms at the end of bridges in Nether Forts, and you can see them pretty easily due to all the yellow Blaze flying around.

Killing Blazes is tricky. You want good gear, preferably some Golden Apples to resist the Blaze's fire attack, some Snowballs and some blocks to build with. Blazes can fly and shoot at you from a distance, so use the blocks to contain the area around the spawner, making it so they can't get out of your range. Snowballs do 3 damage to Blazes and are cheap and easy to throw, so they can be your best weapon against these fiery foes. Use those, Bows and Arrows and the best Sword and Armor you can make, and you should be okay.

When you find the End Portal room, you'll need to deal with this Silverfish spawner first.

Part 3: Opening the End Gate

To open the End Gate, you need to collect a certain amount of items and then find the gate. On the collection side, your first object is to get at least 9 Blaze Rods. One Blaze Rod makes two Blaze Powders, and one Blaze Powder plus one Ender Pearl makes one Eye of Ender. End Portals require 12 Eyes of Ender to open (at the maximum, some already have a few in them), and you'll need a few more in order to actually find the Portal. Additionally, you'll want an Enchantment Table, which takes another Blaze Rod. Add all of that together, and you need at least 9 Blaze Rods.

We've already shown you how to kill Blazes for Blaze Rods above, but you'll also need the Ender Pearls as well, which you get from killing Endermen. This is when the Kill More Mobs section of this guide will come in handy, and you'll probably have to kill quite a few as they don't always drop the Pearls. You should collect at least 16 Ender Pearls, and 20 is even safer.

Give your Portal base everything you can, especially a Bed. You'll probably be dying a few times, so you'll be back here soon.

Once you have your Rods and have made them into Powder (leaving one for your Enchantment Table) and have combined the Powder with the Pearls to make Eyes of Ender, you need to find a Stronghold. This is where your extra Eyes come into play: throw your Eyes of Ender, and they will shoot out toward a Stronghold. You may be able to pick up the Eye again, but they can also break so be careful about not throwing too many (make sure you keep at least 12).

Follow the Eyes, and eventually you'll get to a Stronghold. You'll have to explore the Stronghold, but somewhere in it you will find a room with Lava, a Nether Portal and some Silverfish blocks. Make sure to kill and contain the Silverfish, then build a containment area/ mini-base around the Portal. Finally, activate it by placing the Eyes of Ender into the Portal blocks, and you'll see it kick on!

Part 4: Prep

Now hold yer horses young Crafter: you need to get ready before you dive through that Portal. Besides getting all the best gear you can, you also need to do a few more things before you make the plunge.

- Get the area around your Portal ready. If you die in The End, you just go back to your spawn point in the overworld. Make that mini-base around your Portal and include a Bed that you've slept in and Chests with tons of gear in them. This way when you die, you just gear up again and head right back to The End.
- Take the best gear, and enchant as much of it as is possible.
- In addition to a Diamond Sword or so, bring a Bow and as many Arrows as you can.
- Also bring Potions, a Pumpkin (to wear if the Endermen bother you too much), Water Buckets (to scare off the Endermen), Obsidian, Ladders, Chests and food. This is your kit to beat The End.

Once you've got your base prepared and have everything you need, you're ready to go wreck you an Ender Dragon. Whoo!

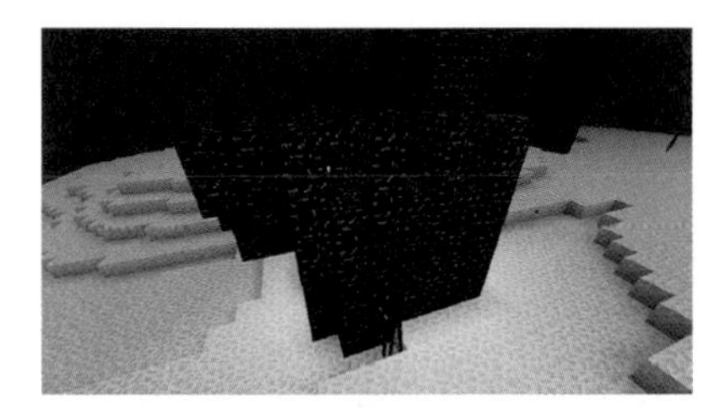

Build a little fort of Obsidian like this in order to survive your attack on the Dragon.

Part 5: Dealing with The End

You'll notice right off the bat that The End is different from the other areas. First thing's first: you need to get off the little area you're floating on and over to the main island. Use Obsidian to build a bridge over, and be careful! The main island is covered in Endermen, not to mention that big ole Ender Dragon flying around.

You can always go straight to the attack, but this isn't likely to get you anywhere but dead unless you are just insanely geared up and good at combat. The best bet for survival and success is, as we so often say in Minecrafter, to control the area.

Use your Obsidian to build yourself a small fort or safe area in The End. Make this so that Endermen can't get in and the Ender Dragon can't see you (so you'll need to make a few layers within it, or some entrance passageways that twist and are too small for the Endermen to get through). The Dragon can't break Obsidian, so you'll be relatively safe to put down resupply Chests in your Obsidian fort, as well as to use it to shoot at your enemies.

Endermen are mostly just pests in The End, so it's best just to kill them quickly or avoid them altogether. Use your Buckets of Water and Pumpkin for this (Endermen won't see you with a Pumpkin on your head, and they hate and are damaged by Water).

Shoot these crystal, Dragon-charger things with arrows if possible, as they explode.

Part 6: Killing the Ender Dragon

Building an Obsidian fort and messin' with Endermen is pretty fun, but you're here for one reason: to kill that big darn Dragon. You'll notice that beams are flying out of those giant Obsidian pillars and touching the Dragon as he flies around: these come out of crystals on the tops of the pillars, and they heal the Dragon. You can't kill him with these still going, as he'll just heal, so you need to take them out.

There are two common methods for this: shoot out the crystals from below with a Bow or Snowballs, or climb the pillars and break the crystals with a Sword. Either method works, though you'll have to be a good shot for the first, and you'll have to deal with the crystals exploding when broken for the second.

Once the crystals are out, attack the Dragon. Enchanted Bows are probably the best weapon here, as you can hit the Dragon when flying, but you can use just about any combat method you want. The keys here are these: have a big supply of the best gear you can get, avoid the fire blasts (they're pretty slow), hide when you need to (in fact, staying in your base and shooting out of it is a great method), and use items like food and potions to keep your health and strength up constantly.

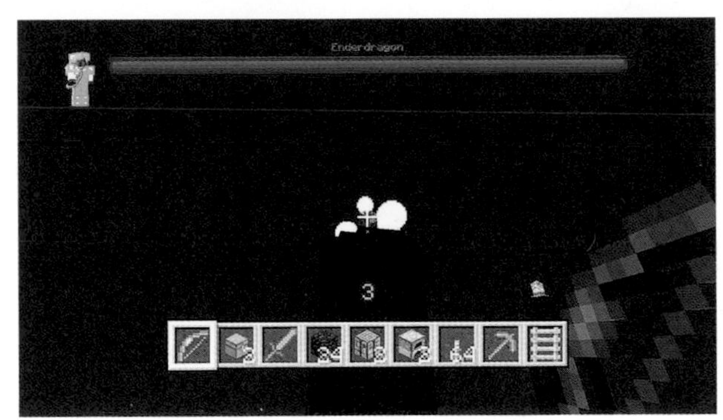

A crystal shatters from a bow shot.

It will be expensive, you will die a lot, and it will take a long time. But when you finally see that health bar drop to nil, and the Dragon starts exploding light everywhere and dropping the craziest amount of experience you've ever seen, you'll know it was all worth it. You've just "beat" Minecraft, brave young Crafter!

Note: Make sure to read the infamous "End Poem" after killing the Ender Dragon. It's a very cool piece of writing, and it'll make you see the game in a different light! It's also one of the only actual "story" parts in the game, so be sure not to miss it.

Minecraft Gallery

Our guide is an excellent tool for getting started on more advanced buildings and concepts, but it's time to show you Crafters what the experts are up to these days. Minecraft really is a game that's limited only by the imagination of the Minecrafter behind the controller (or mouse, or smart phone screen), and the images in this brand-spankin' new gallery showcase some of the brightest and best talents out there in the Crafter world.

In this gallery you'll find soaring castles, sprawling cities, striking homes, dangerous puzzles and even entire worlds created within the game (check out those wild 2b2t shots)! Take a peak, and maybe get you some inspiration for your own new creations and builds. Remember: if it's in these pictures, it was created block-by-block in Minecraft, and there's no reason you can't create something just as awesome.

All it takes is a little thought, a little know-how and a pretty darn big helping of patience. Put those together, and the magic you can create in the game of Minecraft is almost limitless.

SO get to work, Crafters, and who knows? Maybe your creation will show up on the pages of the next edition of Minecraft! We can't wait to see what you guys come up with.

1. Ecclesia Darii by RezolutnyDarek- An ancient cathedral sporting a gorgeous French-style garden in a lush forest; we love this build because it goes so far as to include the landscape as well.

2. Kikoshi Islands by Cephyr- This one is worth a search online, as the entire island is populated with gorgeous cherry blossom trees and a perfectly executed Asian aesthetic.

3. This, oh Minecrafters, is 2b2t. 2b2t is the world's craziest, most dangerous server. It has never been reset, and few players survive even a few minutes before dying.

1
2
3
4
5
6

1. Cliffs of Ferrowyn by Vadact- Like the Kikoshi Islands, this build is detailed. If you have the PC version, you may be able to find this one to download and explore, and we think it's absolutely worth it for its fantastical feel.

2. Puzzlemap 1 by Flying_pig2- The details of this insane puzzle map are not done justice here, but basically every little thing you see here is part of one giant puzzle for players to explore.

3. Imperial City by Rigolo- Using a special software for the PC, this insanely detailed city is seen from above. This is just a fraction of it, too!

4. Wood by Citrus- Texture packs are used in this build to create a gorgeous, almost real modern home. We'd live here!

5. Survival Games by BillTheBuild3r- Not all Survival Games maps take their look from that one movie; this one has a sweet little boat section! We wonder what's about to happen to the big ship in the center. . .

6. World of Keralis by RaptorAnka2- Another full-world build, we can just imagine this city in our favorite fantasy novels.

7. Imperial City by Rigolo- We liked the Imperial City so much, we had to put another shot in! Note the airship just beyond the arch, and that amazing clock tower.

8. Craentich Castle by matei301 and Klint95- Everyone builds castles in Minecraft, but few look this good, or this unique. The blue is a lovely touch, we think.

1. Hillside Manor by inHaze- This build doesn't use crazy mods or insane textures, but we wanted to include something awesome that you could build in your console or Pocket Edition games. The multi-layered deck is inspired, and the diving board is just the perfect touch to break up the repetition.

2. Palace of Isunita by Sunfury- Not just a castle, this is obviously a glamorous palace. Sunfury should be an architect in real life, if he isn't already. Just look at those windows!

3. Olann Island by Enmah- This is actually just one section of a giant, world-covering build, but it's our favorite theme park of any we've seen yet. It actually looks like a real place, and the slides actually work!

4. 2b2t- We had to throw another 2b2t shot in here, as we're fascinated by this anarchic server. At this point in its existence, players had used cheats to spawn huge amounts of stone and lava over the spawn point, which had then been blown up by an unfathomable amount of TNT. 2b2t is still quite active and accessible to any player with a PC, but we warn you: there are no rules on 2b2t, and it can get pretty crazy in there.

5. Unknown Desert Palace by OreoBA- We don't know what this is called, but get on your computer and look up OreoBA right now. If you can, find a hi-res shot of this palace or his other builds; they're in a class of their own. We mean, just look at that design, not to mention that insane render distance (certainly modded).

1

2

6. Winter's Secret by Ignitized- It wouldn't be Minecraft without some insane underground worlds! This one may still be accessible online, and it's an adventure waiting to happen.

7. Frigid by [Colors]- Simple, elegant and totally unique, Frigid is one of the best modern houses we've seen yet.

8. Sacred Worlds: The Wizard's Sanctum by CathonicCraft- It's got two giant towers, a wall like we've never seen, a moat (moats are the best!) and looks straight out of Disney. Five stars to CathonicCraft.

4 5 6

More Ways To Play

1 in 256

Throwing an Egg has a 1 in 256 chance to hatch 4 Chickens at the same time.

So mining's great, exploration's always a hoot and mob huntin' has its place, but every Crafter at some point seeks out a little distraction from the project-making, death-avoiding grind. You'd think that you might have to switch to another game to get some variation in your hard-mining life, and maybe you would with another title, but Minecraft is special. The game's open-ended system gives the opportunity for players to create almost endless variations, mini-games and new ways to play, and we've got a few of the community's best here for you to try out.

We're not sure the crouching helped this Minecrafter, who is about to get tagged by the seeker.

Think you can find players hidden in this Jungle?

Hide 'n Go Brain

The classic game of Hide 'n Go Seek works well in Minecraft with a good arena and players that are willing to stick to the rules. Set up a designated space (like a per-constructed arena or a fenced off part of your map) and make one player "It" while the rest hide for an agreed upon amount of time (a minute or two, usually). The "It" player then attempts to find and kill the other players, who can only move from their hiding spots once "tagged" (attacked) by the "It" player. This can get seriously competitive and creative, especially when you design a nice map with lots of little hiding spots. Tip: Decide whether players can dig or not. Arenas with difficult-to-break borders (Obsidian or even Bedrock) can help with this issue, as digging or destroying the environment becomes an effective finding strategy.

Can you spot the Chest?

Hide 'n Go Grab

Similar to the above, except instead of trying to find other players, you're trying to find specific items they've hidden in chests around the playing field. This game has a different energy to Hide 'n Go Brain, as you can have each player hide an item specific to their character (For instance, Trevor hides a Diamond while Matt hides an Iron Block) and everyone can search at the same time.

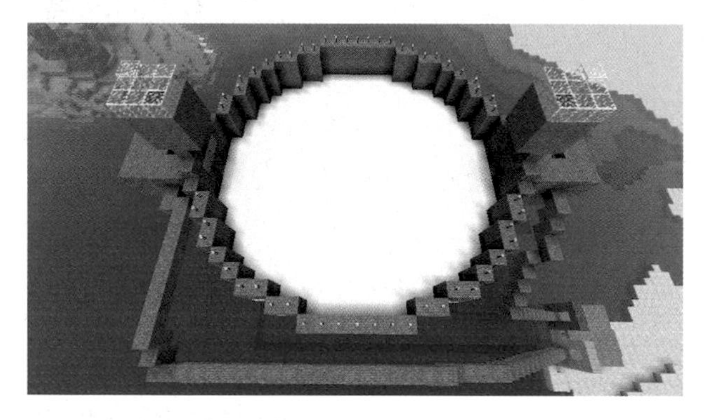

A simpler Spleef arena by stickmanmob. Spleef doesn't need to be hard to build, but you can always add on to your arena later and make it super detailed.

Spleef!

If there's a game that best embodies the player-created competition of Minecraft other than Hunger Games, it's Spleef! Spleef is crazy fun, and it's really not that hard to set up if you have a friend or two.

Spleef's concept is all about the set up, and it's pretty simple: a one-block-thick layer of Wool sits above a pool of Lava in an arena constructed of tough materials (such as Obsidian). Players start on top of the layer of Wool in the corners of the arena and use Flint and Tinder or Fire Charges to light the Wool on fire in the path of the other players. When the Wool burns, it disappears, leaving gaps in the floor through which players can fall. The last player who has stayed out of the Lava wins! There are endless awesome variants on this game, such as including permanent blocks to jump to for safety, incorporating a maze into the arena, adding Ender Pearls to the mix (to teleport around the playing field), using multiple layers of Wool or even putting blocks of TNT here and there to mix things up a bit.

Spleef arenas have become so popular that they're pretty much a genre of structure in Minecraft, so don't hesitate to deck yours out and make it a glorious place for battle.

Variant:

Use hostile mobs and kite or punch them to the finish line. Much more dangerous, not only for you, but also your mob, as you'll lose if they die (or at least have to start over, depending on how hardcore you play).

You might think you could get a Sheep through this maze by Rolf-David, but we promise you; it's harder than it looks.

Lead the Sheep

Skillfully jumping your way through a maze or puzzling out an obstacle course is all well and good as a player, but it takes skill to lead a peaceful mob through a dangerous environment to safety. Maps for this game can be somewhat difficult to perfect, as you need to make sure that the chosen mob can actually maneuver through your course, but when you get this game right, it can lead to some of the funniest and most praise-worthy competitions you'll have in Minecraft.

Players in this competition are striving to build a stack of four Diamond Blocks, which is like, really darn hard.

Stack Buildin'

Want to test how good you are at sniffin' out certain materials? Stack Buildin' is a game that lets you prove that you know yer minin', and it's one of the easiest games to set up as it only requires loading a new seed. Once in, you and the other competitors have to collect four blocks of a certain material, which you then stack in an agreed-upon location on the map. Typically this game is played where the final stack can't be destroyed, but players in-transit can be attacked and robbed with impunity (ain't impunity great).

Watching the other players' stacks grow each time you return to build on your own leads to players frantically searching for that last block of ore, and you'll have to bust out all of your best mining strategies to win. This one has almost endless variations, as you can customize everything from the material needed to the time given to the environment you mine in.

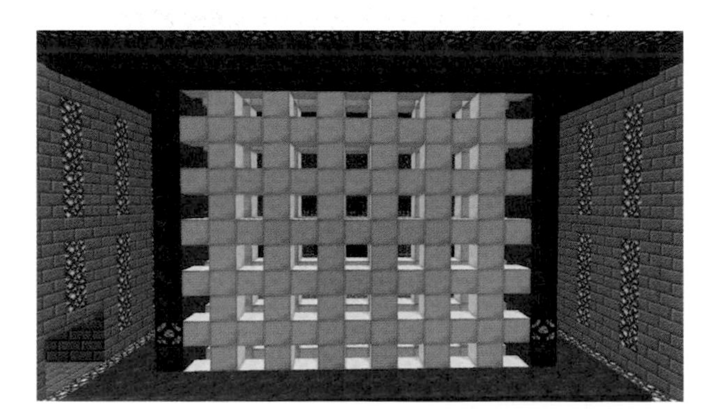

A nice Connect More than Three that uses Redstone, by Geti2.

Connect More than Three

Based on a certain popular game, this Minecraft mini-game is so easy to set up it's just ridiculous. Basically you just create a hole in the wall one block deep and as many blocks wide and tall as you'd like with player access to the top. This is your playing field, on which two players play, with each picking either Gravel or Sand as their material. Players take turns dropping a block of their material into the playing field, stacking the blocks and attempting to Connect More than Three in a row, either vertically, horizontally or diagonally.

Pick a color of Sheep, and start tagging!

Sheep Tagger

Fence off an area (or don't) and give each player 20-50 sheep of their chosen color. Release the sheep, and give the players 5 minutes to run around the map trying to dye as many sheep as they can with their own color. Incredibly fun if you've got a map with some nice caves, waterfalls and other hiding spots, though it can be a bit hard to count. Of course, finding, counting and killin' all of the sheep at the end of the game can be part of the fun too.

The higher you build your leaping platform, the harder it is to hit the target.

Leap of Faith

You'll know in about four seconds if you win this one. Essentially this game is darts, but instead of a dart, you use yourself, and instead of throwing, you fall really far and try not to splat. Set up is simple but can take some time: build yourself a real darn tall tower, cliff or other high spot, and create a target down below with water at its center. You can do concentric rings of water, or make just the bulls-eye safe to land in if you'd rather watch some of the less-accurate types die a bit. The only drawback to this game is havin' to haul yourself back up the ladder to the jumpin' point, but a quick reload or a nice Minecart system can cut the travel time down substantially.

Mobile Minecraft

As of 2014, the PC and console editions of Minecraft still rule the roost, but there's another title in the Minecraft world that has been steadily making headway since its release in 2011: Minecraft Pocket Edition. This byte-sized (excuse our bad pun) version of everyone's favorite building game has been released for the iOS and Android systems, and though it's still significantly behind the other versions of the game in many ways, it's a heck of a lot of fun for just $7. And considering it's still in its "Alpha" phase (meaning it's not considered complete yet), there's a **lot** coming up for this mini-Minecraft version in the next year or so.

Carrots and Beetroot, seen in only Pocket Edition and PC and Pocket Edition alone, respectively.

What's It Like to Play?

Playing on mobile touchscreen platforms like tablets and smart phones is going to be a bit different from the other versions if for no other reason than there being no keyboard or controller to use with the game, and that's the first thing you'll notice when you pick up Minecraft PE. In order to deal with this issue, the folks at Mojang have created a system which utilizes, unsurprisingly, sections of the touchscreen for the movement and viewing controls.

The controls work like this:

Movement: Minecraft PE features a "directional pad" (or d-pad) displayed on the left side of the screen. This basically just looks like buttons with arrows on them that point forward, backward, left, right and diagonally, and you use these to move. (No way right?!)

Lava and more await in the Pocket Edition.

Looking around: This is the part of the controls that might seem a little hard to implement, but Mojang has done a very good job with looking around. When you hold your device to play Minecraft, you hold it horizontally (landscape-style), so your left hand will be on the left side of the device, leaving your left thumb to use the movement controls. Rather brilliantly, your right thumb is what you use to look around, and you do that by touching it to the screen in the bottom right hand corner. You don't have to move your thumb much to look all the way around, making it pretty easy to navigate in the Pocket Edition.

A nice flower garden outside a quaint Pocket Edition home.

Interacting/Placing Blocks: Once again, the touch screen makes this pretty darn easy: all you gotta do to place a block is simply select the block in your tray and then tap where you want it to go. To mine or remove blocks, just hold down on the block you want to snag. When you do this, you'll see a little circle pop up around the block and start to fill in; this is a neat little feature that allows you to see how long it will take to mine the block (something we kinda wish was in the other editions).

Jumping: In order to cut down on the thumb-wear, Mojang decided to make jumping automatic when it comes to moving toward blocks that are higher than the one you're on, but if you need to jump otherwise, simply tap the button in the center of the d-pad.

Another style of Pocket Edition home.

Pocket Edition Features

Players familiar with the other versions of the game will have one big question after the controls: what's different about the Pocket Edition? The quickest answer to that big query is that Minecraft PE has most, but not all, of the blocks and items that are in the console versions, and the terrain is limited to the overworld (no Nether or End) with not as much variation in the landscape (no caves yet).

Here are some of the most significant differences between the console and Pocket Editions of Minecraft:

- Crafting uses a slightly different system, though you still don't have to have "recipes" as you do in the PC edition.
- Worlds are finite at 256 by 256 blocks.
- Default render distance is actually better than in the PC version or Xbox.
- Graphics are similar, but in the PE, shadows move with the sun (something not found in other editions yet).

The Pocket Edition-exclusive Nether Reactor before it's completed.

- There are some items found in the PC version and PE version that are not in the console edition yet: Carrots, Potatoes, Cobblestone Walls, Hay Bales and Carpet.
- Two items (so far) are actually exclusive to the PE, including: the Stonecutter (generates stone blocks), the Nether Reactor (see below), and Beetroot (a food and dye item). Mojang has said that they plan on doing more exclusive items in the future.
- Multiplayer is supported, but requires either a Local Area Network, Minecraft Realms or user-created servers.
- There is no Nether in the PE, but you can build a Nether Reactor. This essentially spawns a type of Nether Fort in the overworld, allowing you to acquire Nether blocks.
- Mobs are somewhat different: there are no Endermen, Cave Spiders or any Nether mobs except Zombie Pigmen, which are naturally hostile to the player and will spawn with the Nether Reactor.
- Caves and many Biomes and Biome features are not yet available.
- Redstone is available, but it does not work as wiring and seems to be mostly decorative for now, other than use with Minecarts.

Coming Up Soon!

This being a Mojang title, there's a ton more to come for Pocket Edition Minecraft. In fact, the update set to come out after the writing of this guide is likely to be huge, adding enough new features to bring the game closer to the console edition than ever.

What we may see soon:

- Caves! And other structures, like Lava pools, Villages and possibly more.
- New mobs, like Endermen and Villagers.
- New Biomes and Tree types.
- Bigger worlds.
- Expanded Redstone mechanics.
- Music!

Keep your eye on the updates as they come out, as Mojang's goal is to eventually bring the PE to at least where the other editions are now, and it looks like they're going to take the biggest steps yet toward that goal in the next few years.

MASTER BUILDER 2.0

ADVANCED

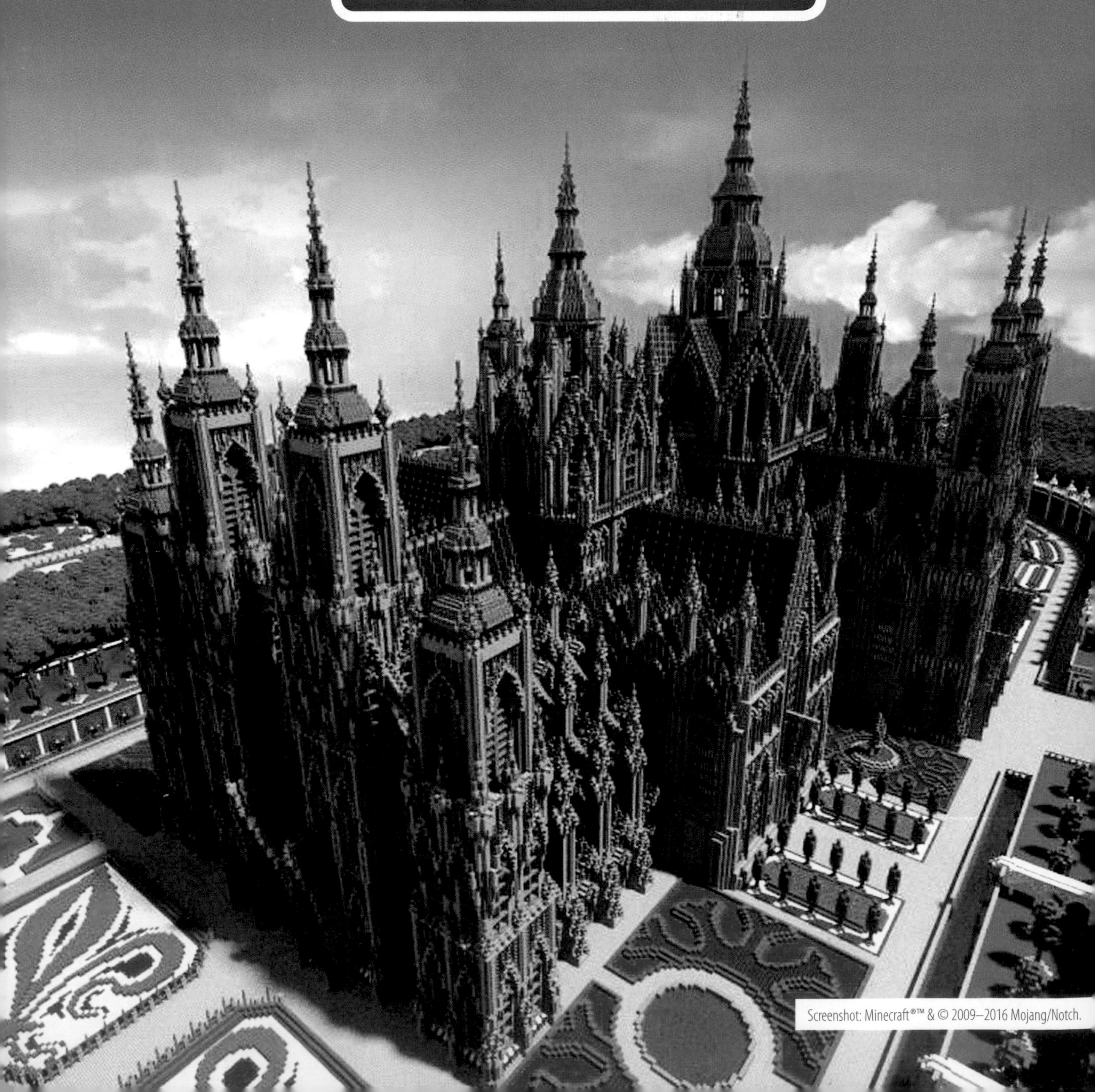